Towards A Functional Competition Policy For India

Pradeep S Mehta (57) is the founder Secretary General of the Jaipur-based Consumer Unity & Trust Society (CUTS), a leading research and advocacy group established in India in 1984. CUTS now operates out of six offices in India, and one each in Zambia, Kenya and UK. Mehta has studied commerce at the Calcutta University and law at the Rajasthan University, Jaipur. Mehta serves on several policy-making bodies of the Government of India, related to trade, environment and consumer affairs. He is the Chairman of the Advisory Board of the South Asia Watch on Trade, Economics and Environment (SAWTEE), Kathmandu, and Co-Chairman of the International Network of Civil Society Organisations on Competition. In the past, he has served on the governing boards of the International Centre for Trade and Sustainable Development (ICTSD), Geneva, Life Insurance Corporation of India, Mumbai, Consumer Coordination Council, New Delhi and on the Global Policy and Campaigns Committee on Economic Issues of Consumers International, London.

He also serves on the advisory bodies of the Manchester University's Centre on Regulation and Competition, and on Loyola University's Institute of Antitrust and Consumer Protection. He is a Visiting Fellow to the Centre on Trade and Investment, Government of Rajasthan. Furthermore, he serves on the WTO Director General's Informal NGO Advisory Body.

Mehta writes extensively in the press in India and abroad, and has published several papers and books, which include: Essays on the International Trading System; Multilateralisation of Sovereignty; Environmental Conditions in International Trade; Analysis of the Interaction between Trade and Competition Policy; State of the Indian Consumer; Numbers at What Cost ? ; and a serial publication: Globalisation and India — Myths & Realities. The last is addressed to the common person in India, which helps to clarify many basic issues about

Towards A Functional Competition Policy For India

AN OVERVIEW

Edited by
Pradeep S Mehta

Published by Academic Foundation, New Delhi
in association with Consumer Unity and Trust Society
(CUTS International), Jaipur

CUTS International

CUTS Centre for Competition,
Investment & Economic Regulation
(C-CIER), Jaipur

Academic Foundation
New Delhi

DISCLAIMER : The views expressed in the book are solely those of the authors and do not necessarily reflect the official position of CUTS or of the organisations to which they are affiliated.

NOTE : For references, readers are requested to refer the second volume of the report, which contains detailed chapters

First published in 2005 by

Academic Foundation
4772-73 / 23 Bharat Ram Road, (23 Ansari Road), Darya Ganj, New Delhi - 110 002 (India).
Phones : 23245001 / 02 / 03 / 04. Fax : +91-11-23245005. E-mail : academic@vsnl.com
www : academicfoundation.com

Published in association with :

Consumer Unity and Trust Society
(CUTS International), Jaipur
www.cuts-international.org

Towards a Functional Competition Policy for India : An Overview
edited by Pradeep S Mehta.

ISBN 81-7188-449-0

Designed and typeset by Italics India, New Delhi.
Printed and bound in India.

Contents

...Contd. ...

Foreword

The adoption of a new competition law in India, in 2002, was a major development in the history of economic policy making in the country. It did not cheer up many in the business as well as economists. The spectre of a continued inspector *raj* started worrying people. Would it not stifle the growth of entrepreneurship and business when the economy had just started showing good results? Will we not get a new avatar of the Monopolies & Restrictive Trade Practices Commission, (MRTPC) which did not exactly play an encouraging role in its heydays? These were some of the questions that were dogging the public discourse.

Theoretically speaking, trade liberalisation is one of the most effective measures to curb abuse of market power and the rent seeking behaviour of business. However, even this has its limits. Imported goods cannot reach the consumers directly, and the well entrenched market players may have a grip over the distribution channels, which may nullify the gains of liberalised trade. Then, there are goods and services which are not tradable. There are goods which are tradable but only within a limited market. Cement, being a classic example of this. Due to its bulky nature, it is not economical to transport it to distant markets. As a result, even geographical segments of a national market can be successfully monopolised or cartelised.

Thus, it is not surprising to see that while countries have gone for more and more trade liberalisation, over the last one decade, more and more countries have also embraced competition laws, with many adopting new laws after scrapping their old ones. In the beginning of 1990, there were about 30 odd countries with a competition law. However, at present, the number is approximately 100 and many more are in the queue. Obviously, there is a greater acceptance of the fact that trade liberalisation may not always be a perfect remedy for an abuse of market power.

In any discussion on the usefulness of a competition authority in India, the performance of the MRTPC cannot be ignored. Expectedly so, as the MRTP Act is being replaced by the Competition Act. Industries still remember MRTP Act, for its negative role, in the pre-reforms era when most big companies would be designated as monopoly companies. The MRTPA would be used to stifle growth of companies.

Given this context, there could not be a more appropriate time for this volume to be published. As a matter of fact I am not aware of any other study that has given such a comprehensive treatment to the issue of competition policy in India. It is a path breaking project. Contrary to popular perception, the study does not treat competition policy as just adoption and implementation of a competition law, but looks at it as a broader policy framework where competition is encouraged as a market process. Thus, it rightly points out that along with the implementation of the Act, government policies need to be appropriately tuned at both central and state levels. The government at the centre has made competition a serious policy issue, therefore, one hopes that the policy makers will take this volume as seriously as it deserves to be taken.

Through sectoral analyses, the study brings out the various dimensions of competition issues, which need to be taken seriously, not only by the competition authority and the governments, but also by different sectoral regulators, and all other stakeholders. An important aspect of the study is that it has looked at regulation, not as an instrument of price control but as a process to bring forth competitive outcomes in a non-competitive situation.

As rightly articulated in the study, the competition policy would require that various institutions function properly, and these include the competition authority, the various branches of the government at centre and the states, along with sectoral regulators. This would require better accountability of all such bodies, which can only become possible if all the stakeholders are aware of the relevant issues. The stakeholders include, in addition to governments and regulators, people in academia, media, trade unions and civil society organisations, particularly the consumer groups. It is thus imperative to build the capacity of all stakeholders.

The report would be useful to all those who are interested in economic policies, in general, and competition policy, in particular. The present volume, through raising awareness and building capacity on competition policy issues, particularly of the civil society, will ensure better accountability of governments and the regulators, and thereby taking care of government failures to a large extent. I am assured, by the fact, that the demand for competition policy and law is coming not from armchair economists and policy makers, but from the consumer movement. I am highly optimistic about this, as this report, rich in analyses of the relevant issues, has come out not from an 'academic' institution, but a consumer organisation.

I must also confess my deep admiration for CUTS and its head: Pradeep S Mehta, the editor of this volume, for their crusade in pushing the system to work in favour of the common people. CUTS is a rare research and advocacy organisation, which works at the grass root to the international levels, simultaneously, on several policy issues. We need more such people and groups to push the reforms agenda, so that our nation constantly rises to higher levels of endeavour and achievement.

— VIJAY L. KELKAR

Chairman, India Development Foundation,
and Former Adviser to Finance Minister,
Government of India

Preface

I do not propose to argue the case for an effective competition policy, and what such a policy could do to address consumer interests. Pradeep S. Mehta has done that very eloquently in the introductory chapter; he has also succinctly summarised all the chapters in the Overview version of the report, in a manner that would persuade readers not only to read the Overview, but look forward to the full report. A conducive climate for the new competition law to be understood, and accepted, is necessary to further economic reforms in India. I am, therefore, not surprised that CUTS, with its commitment to promote competition, and through the process enhance consumer welfare, has brought out this report.

The contributors to this report are researchers, eminent academics and policy makers. I had the privilege of chairing an illustrious Steering Committee which guided the project. I had initially feared that a meeting of such talented and, perhaps, 'argumentative Indians', if one might borrow a phrase from the title of Professor Amartya Sen's forthcoming book, would be one endless debate. My fears were misplaced. They were all so committed to the cause, and so enthusiastic about the project, that each meeting of the steering committee was crisp and productive, and a pleasure to attend. Two stimulating days were spent in the congenial surroundings of the village resort: Chokhi Dhani at Jaipur, where all the papers were presented and critiqued. It was very much like a family gathering to discuss issues that were of common interest. The credit for all this goes almost entirely to Pradeep Mehta and his team of young, bright and energetic professionals at CUTS. Pradeep's enthusiasm and dedication were contagious.

I hope that the new competition authority will soon be in place and will find this report useful, both for advocacy and in shaping its approaches to promote competition in sectors that are of importance to every Indian.

More importantly, I earnestly hope that the report would be used by governments, both at the centre and in the states, to address systemic problems, and to mainstream competition policy in their economic and fiscal policies.

— S. SUNDAR

Distinguished Fellow,
The Energy & Resources Institute,
New Delhi

Acknowledgements

This report was prepared under the supervision of Pradeep S Mehta, and the overall guidance of the Steering Committee, comprising of S. Sundar (Chairman), Shankar Acharya, TCA Anant, Suman Bery, B.B. Bhattacharya, S. Chakravarthy, V.K. Dhall (special invitee), Shubhashis Gangopadhyay, Subir Gokarn, Shrawan Nigam, Manoj Pant, TCA Srinivas Raghavan, S.L. Rao and Pronab Sen.

The foreword has been written by Vijay Kelkar.

The various chapters were written by Manish Agarwal, TCA Anant, Aditya Bhattacharjea, S. Chakravarthy, Ramesh Chand, A. Damodaran, Prabhat Dayal, A.S. Firoz, Shubhashis Gangopadhyay, Sunil Jain, Bharath Jairaj, K. J. Joseph, Amirullah Khan, Devendra Kodwani, Rajeev Mathur, Pradeep S Mehta, Praveen Mohanty, Nitya Nanda, KV Ramaswamy, Jaivir Singh, S. Sundar, and Mahesh Uppal.

Comments on chapters were received from Vivek Agarwal, Sanjeev S Ahluwalia, Diwakar Babu, Laveesh Bhandari, S.S. Bhandare, T.H. Chowdary, Biswanath Goldar, Barbara Harriss-White, Surendra Kanstiya, Rajat Kathuria, K.L. Krishna, Bhanwar Lal, V.K. Mathur, Jiban K Mukhopadhyay, R. Nagaraj, Raghav Narsalay, Anand Pathak, Amit Sengupta, N.S. Siddharthan, Pradeep Srivastava, N. Suresh, Suresh Tendulkar, P.N. Vijay and V.S. Vyas.

The report benefited from participants in a Brainstorming Session in New Delhi in March 2004, a Seminar on Functional Competition Policy for India held in Hyderabad in October 2004 and a Project Review Meeting in Jaipur in October 2004.

Inputs and comments were received during the various stages of preparation from: Pierre Arhel, Nazeeb Arif, T. K. Arun, T. Balachandran, Shantanu Banerjee, A.S. Bhall, T.P. Bhat, T.A. Bhavani, S. Bhattacharya, Philippe Brusick, Malti Chandkika, Bipul Chatterjee, M. K. Chaudhuri, R. Desikan, Dalia Dey, K. S. Galundiya, Reena

George, Pushpa Girimaji, M. Gopalakrishna, Madan Giri Goswami, N. K. Jain, Usha Jumani, Amitabh Kumar, C. V. Kumar, Manoj Kumar, Ujjwal Kumar, Arvind Mayaram, V.D. Maalwade, R. K Mishra, N. L. Mitra, Y.G. Muralidharan, A.K Padmanabhan, Ranjan Panda, Vinayak Pandey, Narendra Pani, S. Peer Mohamed, Sanjib Pohit, K.Y.U Durga Prasad, Marc Proksch, K. Raghu, P. Ravi Sekhara Raju, P.C. Ramakrishnan, A.V. Narasimha Rao, T. K. Rao, Dhanna Singh Rawat, C. Rami Reddy, D. Narasimha Reddy, Amrit Lal Saha, Bhaskar Samvat, S.K. Sarkar, Nabinananda Sen, N. Surya Senthil, U. Shankar, V.B. Shastry, Abhinav Shukla, A.R. Sihag, Harsh Vardhan Singh, Manjit Singh, Lakshmidevi Somnath, Mahendra Soni, K. Srinivasan, K. Swaminathan, G. Narayana Swamy, K.L. Thapar and Arif Waqif

The financial support of the Department for International Development, UK is gratefully acknowledged. Gratitude is also expressed for all the above-named persons for their contribution to the project, and a special thanks to Manish Agarwal, the project manager, S. Sundar for steering the project, and to Vijay Kelkar for writing a most complimentary and encouraging foreword.

Assistance in the project management was provided by Shweta Agarwal, Vikash Batham, Nupur Mehta, Anudeepa Nair, Sheela Rai and Vijay Singh.

Contributors to this Volume

Pradeep S. Mehta	*Secretary General, CUTS International*
S. Chakravarthy	*Former Member, MRTP Commission, Adviser/Consultant on Competition Policy and Law, and Fellow, CUTS Centre for Competition, Investment & Economic Regulation (C-CIER)*
Manish Agarwal	*Policy Analyst, CUTS Centre for Competition, Investment & Economic Regulation (C-CIER)*
Aditya Bhattacharjea	*Reader, Department of Economics, Delhi School of Economics, University of Delhi, Delhi*
Nitya Nanda	*Policy Analyst, CUTS Centre for Competition, Investment & Economic Regulation (C-CIER)*
T.C.A. Anant	*Professor, Department of Economics, Delhi School of Economics, University of Delhi.*
S. Sundar	*Distinguished Fellow, The Energy and Resources Institute (TERI), New Delhi*
Jaivir Singh	*Assistant Professor, Centre for the Study of Law and Governance, Jawaharlal Nehru University, New Delhi*
Prabhat Dayal	*Fellow, CUTS Centre for Competition, Investment & Economic Regulation (C-CIER)*
Rajeev Mathur	*Director, CUTS International*

Bharath Jairaj .... *Legal Coordinator, Citizen consumer and civic Action Group, Chennai*

Ramesh Chand .... *Principal Scientist, National Centre for Agriculture Economics and Policy Research, New Delhi*

K.V. Ramaswamy .... *Associate Professor, Indira Gandhi Institute of Development Research (IGIDR), Mumbai*

A.S. Firoz .... *Chief Economist, Economic Research Unit, Ministry of Steel, Government of India*

Amir Ullah Khan .... *Fellow, India Development Foundation, Gurgaon*

Mahesh Uppal .... *Director, Telecommunications & Computer Information Systems, New Delhi*

Devendra Kodwani .... *Director, Tolani Institute of Management, Kutch, Gujarat*

Sunil Jain .... *Contributing Editor, Business Standard, New Delhi*

Shubhashis Gangopadhyay ... *Director, India Development Foundation, Gurgaon*

Praveen Mohanty .... *Prognosis Capital Advisor, India Development Foundation, Gurgaon*

K.J. Joseph .... *Visiting Senior Fellow, Research and Information System for the Non-Aligned and other Developing Countries (RIS), New Delhi*

A. Damodaran .... *Professor, Indian Institute of Management (IIM), Bangalore.*

1

Introduction

PRADEEP S. MEHTA*

In October 2004, I attended a grand dinner party at Jaipur where people from all walks of life were present. As usual, people were fawning over civil servants, as is the wont. Some of these fellows were quite pleasant, while many strutted around with their noses in the air. Who were the important people who were not there? – the officials of the Department of Telecommunications (DoT)?

Why? A few years ago, telephone officials too strutted around such parties with their noses in the air, because people needed favours from them. For ordinary people like me, we needed a telephone, and one that worked. In any event, after getting a telephone, one would also have to grease the line-man etc., to ensure that it continued to work. Getting through long distance calls was another painful experience. I wonder how many people remember, sometime in the 1980s, when the former Chief Minister of Madhya Pradesh, Mr. P. C. Sethi, walked into a telephone exchange in New Delhi, brandishing a revolver because his trunk calls were not being realised.

What a sea change has taken place! I wonder how many people know the names of the telecom officials in their city any longer, because they don't need to. How many well-connected people make their way into the Telephone Advisory Committees? Hardly anyone, because it doesn't help any longer. Today, one can get different types of telephone services and make calls to anywhere at the drop of a hat. One no longer needs 'approach' to get a telephone connection. A similar story emerges if we look at the air transport sector. Earlier, employees of Indian Airlines too were wooed in order to get seats on over-booked flights. No longer. Now that there is competition, with many private airlines in the country, getting flight seats is no longer a mammoth task.

---

* Secretary General, CUTS International

How does competition help us? Firstly, by ensuring that there are a large number of suppliers, as illustrated above, so that there is rivalry. Secondly, where there are natural monopolies, we require better regulation and price capping, so that we are not exploited. There is huge competition in the telecom sector, which is improving with new technologies available every day. Yet, the sector needs regulation. Rivals can collude, and thus negate the benefits of competition. Or, the tariff plans are made in such a way, that consumers cannot decipher. Thus, there is a Telecom Regulatory Authority of India (TRAI) at New Delhi, which governs the telecom sector including their performance standards.

TRAI is engaged in another area of regulation, which is also quite close to consumers, i.e. Cable TV. In this sector, there are a large number of suppliers i.e. the last mile operator, and a large number of consumers. Yet there is no perfect competition. Here we are stuck with natural monopolies, because they divide the territories among themselves. They too charge exploitative prices. We cannot even change our cable TV operator, as we risk getting no service at all. CUTS has done a nationwide survey on consumer satisfaction, results of which show just how dissatisfied they are. Then there are a huge number of other sectors, such as electricity, where too natural monopolies reign. There are regulatory institutions to govern these sectors, but their capacity is either limited or non-existent. This is made worse, as most regulators are manned with retired bureaucrats or judges, whose whole working life has been under a command and control regime. Their understanding of law and economics in the area of independent regulation is awful. Clearly, we have miles to go.

What is fortunate is that the new government at the centre is very serious about improving competition in the market place, and also to reform the regulatory structure that is in place. Currently, the Planning Commission is engaged in looking at the regulatory infrastructure and seeing how we can bring in best international practices to improve it. Thus, there is intent and the challenge is to convert it into reality.

2005, "Can-Do" Year for India

"I do hope that in the New Year we can all work together to build a more equitable, competitive and humane India.... This is a doable agenda provided

we can set aside our "make-do" attitude and adopt a "can-do" spirit. I want 2005 to be a "Can-Do" Year for every Indian." Dr Manmohan Singh, Prime Minister of India, The Economic Times, December 25, 2004.

This report: "Towards a Functional Competition Policy for India" is dedicated to every Indian, the rich, the not-so-rich and the poor, so that we *can* build a more equitable, competitive and humane India. The process has to start now.

The Prime Minister's exhortation has its roots in the first days of the new government, which has made competition policy a serious issue. Extracted below are the relevant excerpts from the President's Address to the Parliament on June 7th:

> "Revival of industrial growth is of paramount importance. Incentives for boosting private investment will be introduced. Foreign Direct Investment will continue to be encouraged. Indian industry will be given every support to become productive and competitive. Competition, both domestic and external, will be deepened across industry with professionally run regulatory institutions in place to ensure that competition is free and fair.
>
> "The Government will establish a National Manufacturing Competitiveness Council to provide a continuing forum for policy interactions to energise and sustain the growth of the manufacturing industry.
>
> "The Government is committed to a strong and effective public sector, whose social objectives are met by its commercial functioning. But for this, there is need for selectivity and a strategic focus. My government will devolve full managerial and commercial autonomy to successful, profit-making companies operating in a competitive environment.
>
> "My government believes that privatisation should increase competition, not decrease it".

The Common Minimum Programme adds: "It will not support the emergence of any monopoly that only restricts competition. All regulatory institutions will be strengthened to ensure that competition is free and fair. These institutions will be run professionally".

It is in this background, that CUTS' research project endeavours to find out what ails the economy, in the context of competition, and what can be done to improve the situation.

Competition Policy and Other Policies

The main objective of competition policy and law is to preserve and promote competition, as a means to ensure efficient allocation of resources in an economy, resulting in the best possible choice of quality, the lowest prices and adequate supplies to consumers. To put it differently, ensuring competition is just a means to achieve the above-stated objectives. There are complex inter-relationships between competition and other public policies. This factor has a direct bearing on the extent to which competition policy objectives can be pursued without being constrained by or conflicting with, other public policy objectives. Accordingly, even in the absence of a competition law or a stated competition policy, many of the related concerns can be addressed, at least partially, if there are other policies, that are favourable to competition.

Different government policies that may encourage or adversely affect competition, and hence consumer welfare, particularly in the context of the present globalising environment, would include:

- Trade policy
- Industrial policy
- Regional development policy
- Privatisation/disinvestment policy
- Regulatory reform policy
- Fiscal policy
- Intellectual property policy
- Consumer policy
- Labour policy, and
- Environment policy

In addition, sector-specific policies in various areas, such as health, electricity, telecommunications, financial services etc., also affect competition in the economy. Although a competition law may be quite narrow in its scope, competition policy is much more broad and comprehensive in its scope and tries to bring harmony in all government policies that may encourage, or adversely affect competition and consumer welfare.

Promoting Competitiveness Through Competition

Competition policy has a significant role to play in promoting competitiveness and growth. The term 'competitiveness' appears to have aroused considerable controversy in recent years. On the one hand, the word has become a kind of umbrella term for a wide ranging set of policies. On the other hand, the term evokes an analogy, which suggests that nation states compete in the same way that firms compete. It may be true that the nations do not compete but firms do. Nonetheless, it is equally true that while nations may not compete, they may help the firms compete more effectively by following a set of macro policies, which can create an enabling environment. For example, the issue of clearances to set up a business and how long it takes.

A study conducted by the World Bank[1] reveals that in India, entrepreneurs on average go through 11 steps to launch business, which takes 89 days on average, against a regional average of 9 steps and 46 days! In a sample of 145 countries, India was placed at the 130th position in terms of the number of days it takes to get the procedural clearances. What a shame!

The term competitiveness gained wide currency after the introduction of the Competitiveness White Papers in the UK and the European Community in 1994. The backdrop of these white papers was slow productivity growth and decline in relative economic positions of the UK and Europe compared with Japan and the US. The economic malaise of the UK and European economies was thought to be poor competitiveness.

The decline in the UK's (and Europe's) relative economic performance prompted much debate about the appropriate response. In many ways this debate was not new. The UK White Papers on competitiveness start from a recognition of the UK's relative decline, and identify ten policy areas that influence competitiveness. One of these ten areas is the policy related to fair and open markets. Similarly, EU White Papers highlighted four areas for priority action:

- The promotion of investment in intangible assets;
- The development of co-operation between firms;

1. Doing Business in 2004: Understanding Regulation, The World Bank

- Ensuring fair competition; and
- The modernisation of public authorities

Thus we see that both the white papers on competitiveness emphasise the need for ensuring fair competition in the market as an essential ingredient for enhancement and maintenance of competitiveness in the economy. These prescriptions apply to India as well.

Empirical evidence, though focusing mainly on the experience of developed countries, has confirmed that barriers to competition within an economy, whether due to governmental or private restraints, lead to losses in income and welfare. On the other hand, a well-designed and implemented competition policy promotes economic growth by ensuring better allocation of resources, as highlighted by the following examples:

A study carried out for the Australian economy estimates the expected benefits from a package of competition-promoting and deregulatory reforms (including improvements in the competition rules) to incur an annual gain in real GDP of about 5.5 percent, or A$23 billion where consumers would gain by almost A$9 billion besides having an increase in real wages, employment and government revenue.[2]

A report prepared for the UK Government illustrates the benefits of introducing competition into markets in which, previously, it had been absent. The chosen markets were: Retail Opticians, International Telephone Calls, Net Book Agreement, Passenger Flights in Europe, New Cars, and Replica Football Kits. It was found that competition policy led to large price reductions, innovations and product development.[3]

In the context of developing countries, including India, there is a shortage of systematic analyses, regarding the benefits of adopting a competition policy and law. However, a relevant study of the Peruvian competition agency, Indecopi, found that in the first seven years of its operation, the economic benefits due to its operations amounted to

2. http://www.unctad.org/en/docs//c2em_d10.en.pdf
3. The Benefits from Competition: Some Illustrative UK Cases, Centre for Competition Policy, University of East Anglia, May 2004

$120 m against operating costs of $20 m, or six-fold.[4] A study by the Korean Fair Trade Commission, in 2003, found that the benefit (consumer welfare increase and income transfer effect) outweighed the costs (KFTC's budget) of competition law enforcement, in 2000 and 2001, by 34 times[5].

Under the 7Up1 project[6], we found that the Government in India did not appear very serious about the competition regime, as the budgetary allocation to the MRTP Commission was just about 0.0009 per cent of the total government budget, when the ideal budget in other developing and developed countries was in the range of 0.0013 per cent of the total budget. Even a small, poor country like Zambia had provided 0.005 per cent of its total budget to the Competition Commission.

Promoting Effective Markets Through Competition

Competition, though seen as a means of attaining efficiency and fairness, may not necessarily promote these objectives. A perfectly competitive market with many small firms may achieve equality of opportunity (fairness) but may not achieve efficiency, as too many firms will mean that they will not be able to enjoy economies of scale. Obviously, competition policy must deal with trade-offs in its objectives and instruments. This concern has led to a shift from a structural approach to behavioural approach in enforcing competition in market. After all, in a fiercely competitive market, even a duopoly can bring out an outcome that a perfectly competitive market generates. Thus, it may not be necessary to have a highly competitive market structure, provided that appropriate rules of the game can be designed and enforced, so that the behaviour of the market players remains competitive.

This approach may, however, become ineffective when there are natural monopolies, and competition cannot be ensured as such. Situations could also arise where there might be a number of players

4. See Caceres, A (2000), "Indecopi's First Seven Years" in Beatriz Boza, ed., *The Role of the State in Competition and IP Policy in Latin America: Towards an Academic Audit of Indecopi*, Lima.
5. CUTS (2005), "Citizens' Report on the State of Competition Laws in the World", CUTS/INCSOC, Jaipur
6. CUTS (2003), "Pulling Up Our Socks - A Study of Competition Regimes of Seven Developing Countries of Africa and Asia: The 7-Up Project", CUTS, Jaipur.

in the market, but the market itself is so segmented that the individual players become monopolists in the relevant market. The only way to get "competitive outcomes" in such markets is to put in place effective regulation. Thus, regulation in different sectors becomes an integral component of competition policy.

Obviously, competition policy is quite a complex issue. Unfortunately, there has not been much research on competition issues in India. In the past, efforts have been made by the Indian Institute of Management, Ahmedabad, and CUTS, Jaipur. While the IIM-A study did not go beyond policy level, a study by CUTS done under the 7-Up1 Project, revealed a crying need to do further research in some sectors, which display typically anti-competitive behaviour: cement; trucking; services such as cable TV etc.

As the country is poised to implement a new competition law, a lack of understanding of the nature and extent of prevalence of different types of anti-competitive practices in India will pose a major challenge. CUTS has taken up this project to get a better understanding of the competition scenario in India. This will help:

- the government to draft and integrate a national competition policy
- the competition authority to set priorities, and
- other stakeholders to understand the situation and make appropriate interventions.

The project has involved top experts of the country who have good understanding on competition issues, as well as different subjects. Each of their names appear in the relevant chapter. The project was guided by a Steering Committee, comprising eminent experts and economists[7]. The report itself is being published as two separate volumes. This one is an Overview, which principally carries all papers in a précis form, so that a busy reader can go through easily, and get a flavour of what the issues are. The second is a more detailed report, carrying all chapters in greater depth, and is meant for the policy community, particularly the research community. It is also addressed to the more serious policy implementers, including the various branches of the Government, the Planning Commission, the

7. See list at Page 247

Competition Commission of India, and the National Manufacturing Competitiveness Council, the consumer and business community etc., to see what further needs to be done. Both the reports are not detailed research reports, but will serve as curtain-raisers and as a road map for future, more in depth, work.

As an aside, the project had also established an e-discussion group:

FunComp@yahoogroups.com.: This was used regularly to post news and views relating to competition and regulatory issues, which generated debate and thus, better learning among a large economic policy community in India. It also helped the project hugely, by providing inputs. The e-discussion group continues to operate, as a permanent forum for such discussions. Today it has over 200 members, and it continues to grow.

This project has been supported by the Department for International Development, UK as part of a CUTS project: 7Up2, which is engaged in a comparative study of competition regimes in five other countries of Asia: Nepal, Bangladesh, Vietnam, Laos and Cambodia. Part of this project, dealing with the three Mekong countries, has been supported by SECO, Government of Switzerland.

The Report

To begin with, this chapter on Introduction gives an overview of issues covered in the volume. The entire volume is divided into eight parts covering systemic as well as sectoral issues.

Part I brings out India's experience with competition law, and some of the specific challenges that the newly formed Competition Commission of India would face in implementing its mandate.

Evolution of Competition Policy and Law in India (Chapter 2) highlights the economic policy scenario in India before and after the 1991 reforms; the extant competition law—Monopolies and Restrictive Trade Practices Act, 1969; and the evolution of the new competition law—Competition Act, 2002.

What is interesting is that the Monopolies and Restrictive Trade Practices Act, 1969 (MRTP Act) had its genesis in the Monopolies Inquiries Commission, 1965, which had uncovered strong concentration of economic power in various sectors of the economy. Consequently, the MRTP Act was enacted to prevent concentration of economic power, control monopolies, and prohibit monopolistic and restrictive trade practices. Unfair trade practices, a consumer protection provision covering deception, misleading claims and advertising etc, was brought in through an amendment in 1984. However, the MRTP Act was unable to deliver as expected, partly due to the weaknesses in its own structures and composition of the MRTP Commission (MRTPC), but also because it was created at a time when all the process attributes of competition such as entry, price, scale, location, etc. were regulated. The MRTPC had no influence over these attributes of competition, as these were part of a separate set of policies. What a paradox! The MRTP Act was enacted to check the various competition concerns that resulted from the then control regime, but had no say in changing the very elements of that regime.

It was in 1991 that widespread economic reforms were undertaken, and consequently the march, from a "command-and-control" regime to a regime based more on free market principles, commenced. The economic reforms undertaken since the early 1990s significantly changed the economic environment in the country. Major amendments were made to the MRTP Act in 1991, but even these were considered inadequate to deal with the emerging economic order. In view of this, India adopted a new competition law, the Competition Act, 2002 (the Act) to replace the MRTP Act.

Key provisions of the Act are presented in *Competition Act, 2002: The Approach* (Chapter 3). Certain distinguishing features of the Act are noted. For instance, the Act emphasises the behavioural approach to examine competition in the market, as against the structural approach followed by the MRTP Act. Importantly, the Competition Commission of India (CCI) has been given a competition advocacy role, which will help in creating a culture of competition. Other core areas on which the Act focuses are anti-competitive agreements, abuse of dominance, and combinations regulations. One huge gap in the law is its ability to regulate abuse of intellectual property rights, even when it has been recommended in the TRIPs agreement.

A key reason for the ineffectiveness of the MRTP Act was that it was poorly resourced. Hence, for the CCI to play its role effectively, it is imperative to resource it properly, including providing regular training exposure for capacity building of its staff. The second drawback with the MRTPA was its inadequacy in dealing effectively with anti-competitive practices, which was due to lack of definitions, cumbersome procedures and scarce resources. The new law has tried to take care of these handicaps, but the resource issue will depend upon the political will of the government. However, it (would bode well) for the CCI to research some of the critical cases handled by the MRTPC, so that it can approach similar cases with greater confidence and cogency. Some cases could be the cement and tyre cartels, which were never cracked down by the MRTPC.

As part of the 1991 amendments, the MRTP Act was diluted by removing provisions on mergers and acquisitions (M&As), so as to allow unfettered growth. The fourth chapter (*Mergers and Acquisitions in India: Implications for Competition*) looks at the nature of M&As, post 1991 amendments, and shows that merger behaviour of erstwhile MRTP companies was such as it would have come under the scanner of the now diluted MRTP Act. In fact, certain mergers relating to foreign firms involved market shares of a magnitude that would attract the attention of competition authorities in most countries, but in India all M&A activities were beyond challenge, as there is no M&A regulation from competition perspective, since the 1991 amendments. The Competition Act has provisions for combinations regulations, but these will be effective from the third year of its introduction. Firstly, the definition of combinations is very narrow in its scope. It does not include joint ventures, alliances etc. Secondly, the threshold is so high, that many M&As will escape from its scrutiny. For effective M&A regulation, the CCI will have to also monitor those M&As, which are out of the ambit of the Competition Act but, may raise competition concerns.

As India integrates more and more into the global economy, it would become more prone to the anti-competitive practices, operating on a global scale or, originating elsewhere in the globe. *Cross-border Competition Issues* (chapter 5) addresses such issues and highlights the relevant provisions in the Competition Act, in particular that the Act has extra-territorial jurisdiction and embodies the 'effects doctrine'. To make these provisions effective, the CCI would require substantial capacity building. It is suggested that efforts should be made to promote international cooperation at different levels: bilateral, regional and multilateral, to tackle cross-border competition challenges.

Over the years, especially after economic reforms were initiated in the early 1990's, various sectoral regulators, such as in power and telecommunications have been established to attract private investment and create a predictable environment through the establishment of independent agencies. These regulators are also required to ensure healthy competition in the regulated sector. This can lead to overlaps with the competition law. However, we did not have any major problems until now, as our new competition authority has, more or less, been ineffective. So has been the case with some of our regulators as well. However, it is expected that the new competition authority, and the regulators, will be more active in the years to come. This may result in conflicts. Chapter 6: *Interface Between Regulation and Competition Law* has tried to identify potential areas of conflict. It has also made an effort in offering some solutions, based on a study of different jurisdictions, where problems arose and appropriate solutions found out.

The chapter on M&As brings out one such issue of overlapping jurisdiction, which relates to M&A regulation. Besides the CCI, there are other agencies which regulate M&As, such as the Telecom Regulatory Authority of India, Electricity Regulatory Commissions (federal as well as state level), Reserve Bank of India, Securities and Exchange Board of India, company benches of the high courts, etc. However, the objective of regulating M&As varies across these agencies. Proper coordination mechanisms would be required between the CCI and all other agencies, for an effective regulation of M&As in the country.

There are complex inter-relationships between competition and other public policies. Government policies such as trade policy, industrial policy, regulatory reforms, etc. may encourage or impede competition and hence consumer welfare. Thus, although a competition law may be quite narrow in its scope, competition policy is much broader and comprehensive, and seeks to bring harmony in all the Government policies. Part II of the volume traces this interface between competition and various policies of the government, both at the federal level as well as state level.

Central Government Policies: Interface with Competition Policy Objectives (Chapter 7) shows that as policy outcomes are sought to be generated, it is a persistent practice in India to do so, without taking into cognisance that policies need to be framed and implemented in harmony with the market process, and not in a manner so as to stall the process. This is true of both the pre-1991 control regime and even the liberalised regime followed since early the 1990's. Several examples of policies in the current economic milieu are provided, which are not in harmony with the market processes.

Besides Central Government policies, there are policies/practices or regulatory failures of state governments, which lead to anti-competitive outcomes. Unfortunately, these issues are most often ignored, partly because of lack of awareness and partly due to vested interests. Chapter 8 on *State Government Policies and Competition,* does a survey of five such issues, *viz,* procurement policy, excise policy, truck operations, bid rigging in construction contracts, and retail services. Anti-competitive practices are rampant at the state-level and we need state-level competition agencies, backed by appropriate laws, to tackle them. In fact, by promoting competition, the state governments can protect consumer interest as well as increase their revenues.

The two chapters in Part II suggest that all laws and government policies should be assessed on the touchstone of competition. Governments at the federal and the state-level should frame and implement policies by acknowledging the market process. One good way to do it is through a systemic 'competition audit' of all policies, new and old.

Among other goals, Competition Policy aims to promote consumer welfare, mainly in terms of lower prices, better quality of goods and services, more choice, and easy availability. Part III of the volume highlights this aspect of competition policy.

Competition Policy and Consumer Welfare (Chapter 9) highlights that competition policy and law is just one of the tools in the larger context of other overarching public policies, and approaches, that need to be addressed for promoting consumer welfare. In the Indian context, besides the MRTP Act, an important central legislation to provide for the protection of interests of consumers, is the "Consumer Protection Act, 1986" (COPRA). Both the outgoing MRTPA and the COPRA have similar provisions, particularly in the area of unfair trade practices (UTPs). However, the Competition Act, 2002, does not have provisions relating to UTPs, which henceforth will fall within the ambit of only the COPRA.

The chapter presents the experience, with the working of the MRTP Act and COPRA, in terms of protecting consumer interest. It is suggested that progressive legislations need to be encouraged to check market abuses and enhance consumer welfare. To help consumers, either directly or through policy interventions, it is imperative to create and sustain a strong civil society movement.

For the new competition authority to become popular, without which it may face many hurdles thrown in by vested interests, it is necessary that it creates a public buy-in. It cannot do so by addressing only esoteric problems, such as cartels in the transmission tower industry, etc. Not that it is unimportant to demolish cartels, which seem to pervade all our intermediate goods sectors. However, for getting a pro-people image, one way forward for the CCI is to take up systemic consumer abuses, which are ubiquitous at the local level. It could also do so in collaboration with the redressal agencies under COPRA, as retail level competition issues are covered under COPRA. Chapter 10: *Competition Abuses At Consumer Level: Study of Select Sectors*, has laid out a preliminary study of two consumer-level sectors—health services and school education, to see how the prevailing anti-competitive practices at grassroot level are affecting the ordinary consumers.

So far, the report has addressed systemic and cross-cutting issues. In the subsequent parts, we take up sector-specific studies.

Part IV of the volume brings out competition concerns in the primary sector, and discusses the issue of marketing of agriculture produce. In agriculture markets (Chapter 11, *Agriculture Markets in India: Implications for Competition*), there is a huge gap between the prices consumers pay and the prices farmers actually receive. This is because of the chain of intermediaries between consumers and farmers, who most often collude. In a country where two-thirds of the population draws their livelihood directly from agriculture, the linkage between market imperfections, in agriculture goods, and poverty is manifest.

Alternative avenues, for sale and purchase, through cooperative marketing agencies are found to dilute market power of private trade, to some extent. In order to provide more competition at the retail level, and to benefit consumers and producers, innovative marketing mechanisms like *apni mandi* and producer's sales counters, in consumer centres, should be promoted.

In the next part (Part V), we look at competition issues in the manufacturing sector, in general, as well as cement, steel and pharmaceuticals sectors in particular.

Chapter 12, *State of Competition in the Indian Manufacturing Industry,* makes a preliminary assessment of the extent of competition in markets in the 1990's based on available evidence. It looks at changes in market concentration, impact of import competition and FDI, and price and profitability trends. What comes to the fore is that both domestic as well as foreign owned firms have taken dominant positions in many industries. Market concentration has risen in several industries as a consequence. The chapter highlights the need for developing a reliable and consistent data base. Linkage between industry, trade and FDI data needs to be established, and maintained, on a continuing basis. This would facilitate further in-depth studies.

The next three chapters look at specific sectors in the manufacturing sector. Cement (Chapter 13, *Competition Issues in the Indian Cement Industry*) is a basic good that is used mainly in infrastructure, and hence its availability at competitive prices is very important for developing countries. However, because of its bulky nature, the cement industry is very often insulated from outside competition. World over, it has gained notoriety for collusive practices. India is no exception. Indeed, cases were lodged with the competition authority a couple of times. But nothing came out. This is despite the fact that cartelisation in the Indian cement industry is an open secret. The weak provisions in the MRTP Act, along with weak investigation capacity due to resource constraints, among other extraneous factors, are the primary reasons for cartel formation going unchecked for years. The new law is a significant improvement in this regard with clearer provisions and leniency programmes. Careful analysis of offers by different companies, in Central and state government bids, can give important clues if there have been patterns of systematic rotation of winning bids, stable shares of companies in overall procurement, etc. This information would also be helpful in detecting collusive behaviour in the market as well.

Crying hoarse over the shenanigans of the steel industry, the Union Steel Minister Ram Vilas Paswan, has been threatening to set up a steel regulator. It is not a workable proposal, because nowhere in the world is there an independent regulator for any commodity. The only exception is pharmaceuticals, which is usually governed by a regulator, but that too under the relevant ministry. Independent regulation is used for the service sector mainly. The next chapter (Chapter 14) *"Competition Scenario in the Indian Steel Industry"* examines the history of evidence of collusive practices in the steel industry. Needless to say, no action could be taken in this sector too. The structure of the study is more or less on the same pattern as the cement sector.

The pharma retail trade has been exploiting the hapless Indian consumer by colluding, and gouging the industry by squeezing out ridiculous commissions. Chapter 15, *Competition Policy for the Pharmaceuticals Sector in India,* shows that in this sector, it is not only the industry, but the trade is a bigger culprit. It is difficult to promote and maintain competition because of the peculiarity of the pharmaceuticals market, in the sense that consumers do not decide their purchases. There is a need for an effective regulatory framework to promote good prescribing behaviour among the doctors, and to curb collusive/rent-seeking behaviour of the pharmacists. Mergers and Intellectual Property Right (IPR) related abuse of dominance are likely to raise competition concerns in coming years. There is a need to study the behaviour of the bulk drug market and, if desirable, there can be further decontrol in this regard.

Infrastructure is a critical determining factor to achieve and sustain a high growth rate. However, poor and inadequate infrastructure continues to remain a major obstacle. To boost investment in the infrastructure sector, and ensure good quality and accessible services, the Central Government has resolved to create a regulatory framework that is transparent; independent of Government and, provides an impartial balance between public sector and private sector suppliers, and is based on international best practices. Besides, the Planning Commission has been asked to prepare a policy paper indicating what the regulatory structure should be, for each infrastructure area. Part VI of the report takes up three infrastructure areas: telecommunications, energy, and transportation.

The telecom sector is widely recognised as a success story of regulation and competition in India. The number of telephone lines, per person, has grown almost ten fold in the last decade. This is partly due to the advent of private players in the market. However, competition and investment, though present, is yet to be seen in fixed line services, which are used by the majority of households, even as mobile phones now outstrip fixed lines in number. There are several barriers to entry, in these latter services, where benefits of incumbency are largest. It is here that BSNL, the state-owned enterprise, rules the roost. The existing regulatory regime has been largely unsuccessful in controlling BSNL's market power, and regulating it effectively. The fact that BSNL is wholly government-owned also provides important clues to the reason for the failure to regulate BSNL effectively. 'This reason' is the conflict of interest that government and regulators face, in taking decisions, that will impact BSNL's in the market place (Chapter 16, *Competition Issues in Telecommunication Sector*)

In India, Government still dominates most of the primary, as well as secondary, energy sectors at large, though a beginning has been made to allow the private sector in the area. Chapter 17, *Competition and Regulation in Energy Sector in India*, brings out that issues of regulation and competition policy are complex in the energy sector. Any piecemeal approach, to policy formulation or implementation, would delay the development of competitive markets. A cohesive view of competition in the entire energy sector is missing, so far. Recently, there were reports that the government is working towards developing a comprehensive energy policy. In such a case, it would be interesting to observe how much importance is given to make the sector competitive. It is advisable that keeping the bigger picture in mind, the choice, between economic regulation *versus* competition, be examined very carefully.

While the transport sector has grown at a healthy rate of 10 per cent a year during the last decade, this is the sector that has the greatest possibility to hold back India's GDP growth target of 8 per cent. Despite several efforts made by the government, the sector remains inefficient. The reason for this sorry state of affairs eventually boils down to policies that inhibit competition, and their poor regulation in the various transport sectors, as disclosed by Chapter 18, *Competition Issues in Transportation Sectors*.

In the case of the ports sector, for instance, despite allowing the private sector to invest in major ports, there are few instances of this happening, as it is up to the port authority (the Government) to decide to allow competition. It is worse in the case of the railways. They are the primary medium for transporting containers across the country's vast hinterland, and enjoy a total monopoly over this through the Container Corporation of India (Concor). In the aviation sector, similarly, the Government is just about to allow private airlines to fly abroad, but the barriers to entry are still high while the policy is loaded against the public sector carriers. Goods transport by road is often at the mercy of a cartel of transport operators, who, through collusion, dictate rent-seeking freight rates. The chapter argues that whatever needs to be done in the transport sector, to make it more competitive has to be done by way of policy reforms. Since transport is inter-modal, creation of a single, super-regulator could also be explored.

Part VII covers competition issues in services.

Competition and Regulation in Financial Services (Chapter 19), focuses on issues relating to regulatory bodies and regulation. Regulatory bodies exist in the financial services sector because of the fact that markets may fail. Given that entities in the financial sector are taking up several activities related to different markets in the financial sector, for example, banks that are becoming universal banks; there is need to move away from sectoral regulation to functional regulation, i.e. more coordination is required amongst the various sectoral regulators in the financial market. The chapter argues that a change is required in the regulatory mindset, and suggests the appointment of a super-regulator for the whole financial sector. There is also a need to build the capacity of the regulatory authorities to deal with the changing environment of the global financial system.

The key objective of regulators is to address the original source of market failure, which may or may not be, promoting competition, as lack of competition may not be the source of market failure in the first place. However, competition plays an important role in regulated sectors. Chapter 20 (*Competition and Professional Services*) presents a case study of professional services in this regard.

The chapter focuses on three professions: accounting, law and medicine. Due to the idiosyncratic nature of the services provided, the sector is characterised by asymmetries of information. Certain characteristics of regulatory design in professional services, from the point of view of competition, are highlighted. For example, entry conditions are required to ensure that the practitioner is well qualified. The risk involved is that, if the profession is captured, then we may end up in a situation where the entry condition is also used to maintain market return. Restriction on advertisements protects incumbency advantages, as somebody who is well established in a profession gets a huge advantage through word of mouth. It is suggested that the CCI should engage in deeper study through public hearings etc., and a dialogue with professional regulatory authorities for better market practices. Alternatively, co-regulation can be encouraged to discipline self-regulated professions. State-level competition and regulatory agencies can be established *inter alia* to enforce standards of professional conduct, *vis-a-vis* competition concerns. Managing the professions through New Delhi-based bodies is a sub-optimal experience.

Both the Information Technology and Biotechnology sectors are emerging sectors in the economy. It is widely believed that these two sectors have been doing extremely well. The last part (Part VIII) of the volume analyses the two sectors.

Chapter 21, *Competition Issues in Information Technology Sector*, reveals that, during the last decade, India has emerged as a major player in the field of information technology. The analysis shows that in the case of hardware, the removal of tariff barriers and the presence of a large unbranded market, act as sources of increased competition. However, the situation appears to be different in the case of software. The high market concentration in some of the software segments, especially in the operating system, seems to not only have the effect of making software high-priced, but also dampens the development of applications software, on account of the lack of access to source codes. The chapter underscores the need for creating a more competitive environment in the software sector, *inter alia*, by promoting open source software. In this context, it argues for an active state role, to provide appropriate incentives for the promotion of open source software, and create demand by promoting its use in all the e-governance projects. From the hardware side, innovations like 'simputer' need to be encouraged so that hardware becomes more affordable, and leads to greater demand.

Chapter 22, *Implications of Competition Policy on Biotechnology Industry in India,* highlights that India's fast growing biotech sector has the potential of serious implications on the competition environment in the country. However, a constellation of pro-active legislations serves to ensure that competition is not impaired. India's IPR regimes, whilst affording protection to inventions that fulfil the criteria of novelty, non-obviousness and commercial application, do still carry with it the elements for regulating anti-competitive behaviour, on the part of the firms concerned. The flexibilities inherent in India's IPR regimes, coupled with bio-safety, biodiversity, and stringent food safety laws, could go a long way in promoting the biotech sector in a manner that is sustainable and economically advantageous.

In brief, the volume brings out that there is a need to frame a National Competition Policy for the country, so that Government and other economic regulatory agencies are aware and take into account, the competition dimension in their own policy formulations and implementation.

The role of the government needs to be rationalised to promote effective markets. Also, a 'competition audit' of all new and old policies will help the government to promote competition.

Furthermore, there is an imperative need to create State-level competition and regulatory agencies to resolve local problems. Even with regional offices, federal bodies cannot be effective, as has been seen in the case of the MRTPA.

The Competition Commission should be made accountable, through independent review, by consumer organisations, external agencies and peer review by competition authorities from other countries.

Additionally, the consumer movement in the country needs to be adequately resourced and strengthened, to enable the competition and regulatory agencies to perform their tasks and their advocacy roles.

Part I

Competition Law in India

2

Evolution of Competition Policy and Law in India

S. CHAKRAVARTHY*

Introduction

For almost half a century since attaining Independence in 1947, India adopted and followed, policies comprising what are known as "command-and-control" laws and regulations. The competition law of India, namely, the Monopolies and Restrictive Trade Practices Act, 1969 (MRTPA) was one such.

It was in 1991 that widespread economic reforms were undertaken and consequently, the march from "command-and-control" regime to a regime based more on free market principles commenced. The economic reforms undertaken since the early 1990s significantly changed the economic environment in the country. The MRTPA was considered inadequate to deal with the emerging economic order. In view of this, India adopted a new competition law, the Competition Act, 2002 (Act, for brief) to replace the MRTPA.

Development Strategy and the MRTPA

India had adopted the strategy of planned economic development since the early 1950's. Government intervention and control pervaded almost all areas of economic activity in the country. The government determined the plant sizes, location of the plants, pricing in a number of important sectors, and allocation of scarce financial resources. Further interventions were characterised by high tariff walls, restrictions on foreign investments and quantitative restrictions. Competition in the market was thus under severe fetters.

---

* Former Member, MRTP Commission, Adviser/Consultant on Competition Policy and Law, and Fellow, CUTS Centre for Competition, Investment & Economic Regulation (C-CIER)

The system of controls restricted the freedom of entry into industry, and led to concentration of economic power in the hands of a few individuals or business groups. This emergence of monopolistic industries and the indulgence by industrial groups, in restrictive trade practices, were detrimental to the general public. During this time, three enquiries/studies were conducted, which acted as the lodestar for the enactment of the MRTPA.

The first study was by the Hazari Committee, which studied the industrial licensing procedure under the Industries (Development and Regulation) Act, 1951. The second study was by a Committee chaired by Professor Mahalonobis, which studied the distribution and levels of income in the country, and noted that the top 10 per cent of the population cornered as much as 40 per cent of the income. The third study, undertaken by the Monopolies Inquiry Commission (MIC), was presented in October 1965. The MIC noted that there was concentration of economic power in the form of product-wise and industry-wise concentration, and that large-scale restrictive and monopolistic trade practices existed in the market. As a corollary to its findings, the MIC drafted a Bill, which provided for the control of monopolies and prohibition of monopolistic and restrictive trade practices, when prejudicial to public interest.

The MRTP Act, 1969

Following the report of the MIC, the MRTPA was enacted in 1969 and enforced from June 1, 1970. The Act drew its inspiration from the mandate enshrined in the Directive Principles of State Policy in the Constitution, namely, prevention of concentration of economic power.

The thrust of the MRTP Act was directed towards:

- the prevention of concentration of economic power to the common detriment;
- the control of monopolies;
- the prohibition of monopolistic trade practices (MTPs);
- the prohibition of restrictive trade practices (RTPs); and
- the prohibition of unfair trade practices (UTPs) (post-1984 amendments)

One of the main goals of the MRTPA was to encourage fair play in the market, besides promoting healthy competition. In the MRTPA, the basis of determining dominance was whether an undertaking had a share of one-fourth or more in the production, supply, distribution or control of goods or services.

The MRTP Commission

Under the MRTPA, a quasi-judicial authority called the MRTP Commission (MRTPC, for brief) was set up to deal with offences falling under the statute. The Commission was assisted by the Director General of Investigation and Registration for carrying out investigations and for undertaking carriage of proceedings, during the enquiry before the MRTPC.

The powers of the MRTPC included the power vested in a Civil Court, and included further powers such as to—pass a cease and desist order, grant temporary injunction, award compensation and recommend to the Central Government division of undertakings or severance of interconnection between undertakings, if their working was prejudicial to public interest.

The law provided for *suo motu* action on the part of the MRTPC, if it received information from any source or on its own knowledge.

Economic Reforms and Impact on the MRTP Act

In the command and control regime, the market suffered from little or no competition resulting in detriment to economic efficiency and productivity. Cost reduction was neither discouraged nor encouraged. Self-reliance was synonymous with import substitution and consequently, indigenous availability criteria ensured automatic protection to domestic producers regardless of cost, efficiency and comparative advantage.

It was in 1991 that India embarked on liberalisation and economic reforms. A number of changes were introduced in policies relating to industrial licensing, foreign investment, technology imports, government monopolies and ownership, price and purchase preferences for the public sector, reservations for the small scale sector, financial sector, etc. The main objective was to make the market driven by competitive forces, so that there could be incentives for raising productivity, improving efficiency and reducing costs.

The concept of size and monopoly thus changed and resulted in amendments to the MRTPA in 1991. Two of the five thrust areas mentioned above, namely: prevention of concentration of economic power to the common detriment; and control of monopolies, were de-emphasised.

Prior to the 1991 amendments, the MRTPA essentially was implemented in terms of regulating the growth of big size companies, the monopoly companies. Post-1991 amendments; provisions relating to concentration of economic power and pre-entry restrictions with regard to prior approval of the Central Government for establishing a new undertaking, expanding an existing undertaking, amalgamations, mergers and takeovers of undertakings, were all deleted from the statute.

With the restructuring of the MRTPA through the 1991 amendments, the thrust thereof was on curbing monopolistic, restrictive and unfair trade practices. Size, as a factor to discourage concentration of economic power, had been, in a manner of speaking, given up.

Experience with the Working of the MRTPA

i) *Disposal of Cases:* Very few cases relating to monopolistic trade practices (MTPs) came up before the MRTPC, during the nearly 35 years of the MRTPA's existence. None ended in any decision, as most of them were stayed by the Judicial Courts. The MRTPC had, nonetheless, been successful in dealing with cases relating to RTPs and UTPs.

ii) *Anti-competitive Practices:* A perusal of the MRTPA shows that there was neither a definition nor even a mention of certain offending trade practices, which were restrictive in character. Some of the anti-competitive practices like cartels, predatory pricing and bid-rigging were not specifically mentioned in the MRTPA. However, the MRTPC, over the years, had attempted to fit such offences under one or more of its provisions, by way of interpretation of existing provisions.

iii) *Budget for MRTPC:* The budget of the MRTPC, analysed for 1996-1999, was a very small percentage of both the GDP and the budget of the Central Government. Further, in a comparison of nine countries, including India, done by CUTS, in terms of the budget of the Competition Authority as a percentage of the total Government budget, it was found that all other countries had a larger proportion than India. The inadequacy of the budget allocation by the Government is compounded by the need for the MRTPC to seek the Government's permission to incur expenditure, beyond certain limits.

iv) *Autonomy and Independence:* Sanction for most posts, at the senior level of the MRTPC, had to be given by the Government. The autonomy of the MRTPC stood impaired, to a great extent, because of these constraints. Nonetheless, the MRTPC was independent in discharging its investigative and adjudicatory functions. It is worth mentioning that Government had the discretion in the appointment of the Chairman and Members of the MRTPC, which undermined its independence. In this context, the bar on the Chairman and the Members of the MRTPC for seeking appointment in any undertaking, which fell within the ambit of the MRTPA for a period of five years after demitting office, was designed to impart integrity to the functioning of the MRTPC.

The MRTPA, however, was unable to deliver as expected, in part due to the weaknesses in its own structures and composition of the MRTPC, but also because it was created at a time when all the process attributes of competition, such as entry, price, scale, location, etc, were regulated. The MRTPC had no influence over these attributes of competition, as these were part of a separate set of policies.

Metamorphosis from MRTPA, 1969 to Competition Act, 2002

When the MRTPA was drafted in 1969, the economic and trade milieu prevalent at that time constituted the premise for its various provisions. Subsequently there had been a sea change in the policy milieu with considerable movement towards liberalisation and economic reforms. The law had to yield to the changed and changing scenario on the economic and trade front. This was one important reason for the framing of a new competition law.

Following the setting up of the WTO Working Group to study issues relating to the interaction between Trade and Competition Policy, the Ministry of Commerce, Government of India, in its turn, set up an Expert Group on interaction between Trade and Competition Policy. The Expert Group recommended a need for an appropriate competition law to promote fair competition and to control, if not eliminate, anti-competitive practices in the market.

In October 1999, the Government of India appointed a High Level Committee on Competition Policy and Competition Law to advise a modern Competition Law for the country, in line with international developments, and to suggest a legislative framework, which would entail a new law or appropriate amendments to the MRTPA. On the basis of the recommendations of the Committee, a draft competition law was prepared and presented, in November 2000, to the Government. After considering the recommendations of the Standing Committee and effecting some refinements, the Parliament passed the new law, the Competition Act, in December 2002.

To sum up, the factors that gave rise to the metamorphosis from MRTP Act, 1969 to Competition Act, 2002 and that influenced the shape of the new law are:

- The recommendations of the Expert Group (1999).
- The recommendations of the High Level Committee (2000).
- The near unanimity among those who deposed before the High Level Committee for repealing the MRTPA and substituting it with a new competition law.
- Appreciation of the fact that the MRTPA was more concerned with curbing monopolies rather than with promoting competition.
- Appreciation of the fact that the MRTPA was enacted during the pre-1991 control regime and that a new law was needed for the post-1991 liberalising and globalising regime.
- The recommendations of the Standing Committee of the Parliament, and
- Recognition that Indian undertakings are small in size and need to merge and grow to become competitive globally (thus leading to the prescription of fairly high threshold limits for combinations regulation).

One landmark step taken in developing the new law, was the wide consultations on the same, through a Concept Bill. This was placed on the website of the Department of Company Affairs. Even the Parliamentary Standing Committee held meetings in Mumbai and Delhi, with all stakeholders, to firm up their own recommendations.

The new law provides for a modern framework of competition. It deals with three areas: (i) anti-competitive agreements; (ii) abuse of dominant position; and (iii) combinations regulations (combinations include Mergers, Amalgamations, Acquisitions and Acquisitions of Control). The emphasis has shifted from a structural to a behavioural approach to competition. Dominant positions are not prohibited *per se*, but rather their abuse will come under the scrutiny of the competition agency. The regulation of combinations has returned to the scope of Indian competition law, although the new law sets rather high turnover thresholds for combinations to fall under the purview of the Act. The new law no longer covers unfair trade practices (UTPs), and all pending cases are to be transferred to the Consumer Protection Act, 1986 (COPRA), which covers UTPs.

Role of Third Parties

Both the MRTP Act, 1969, and the Competition Act, 2002, provide for third parties to bring action before the Competition Authority. Both the statutes permit any person, consumer, consumer association or trade association, to file a complaint before the MRTP Commission or the Competition Commission of India, as the case may be. Thus, challenge to any anti-competitive agreement or to abuse of dominance or to combinations, is available to third parties. It is hoped that consumer associations and consumer activists will act as a watchdog on competition in the market, and invoke the provisions of the Act, where necessary, in the larger interest of consumers.

Consumer Protection Act, 1986 (COPRA)

Besides the MRTPA, an important central legislation to provide for the protection of interests of consumers is the "Consumer Protection Act, 1986" (COPRA). Its sole concern is the welfare of the consuming public. It is supplementary to and not in derogation of the MRTP Act/ Competition Act. It can be said to be an offspring of the consumer movement in India. COPRA has provisions for the establishment of consumer disputes redressal fora for the settlement of consumer disputes. Quasi-judicial machinery has been set up at the District, State and Central levels, empowered to give relief to the consumers and to award compensation for the loss or injury suffered by them. Each has a monetary limit and hears appeals against the lower fora, while the Supreme Court is the ultimate arbiter.

Both the outgoing MRTPA and the COPRA have similar provisions, particularly in the area of unfair trade practices. Where the area of jurisdiction overlaps, the complainant has the option to choose either of the fora for seeking redressal of his/her grievances. As noted above, the Competition Act, 2002, does not have provisions relating to UTPs, which henceforth will fall within the ambit of only the COPRA.

With the coverage of UTPs being only with the consumer fora after the Competition Act, 2002 is brought into force, COPRA has also been amended to include the power of granting temporary injunctions. Earlier COPRA had powers to grant relief to the complainants on post facto complaints, without the power of injunction. This was now necessary, as without it, the urgent issues which are causing harm to consumers, could not be stopped.

Sectoral Regulatory Authorities

Over the years, especially after economic reforms were initiated in the early 1990s, a number of sectoral regulatory authorities have been formed. For telecommunication, there is the Telecom Regulatory Authority of India (TRAI) and an appellate tribunal. For electricity, there is the Central Electricity Regulatory Commission (CERC) at the federal level and the State Electricity Regulatory Commissions (SERC) in most States. There are other statutory bodies for regulating some other sectors, and some more are in the offing (e.g. petroleum).

Regulatory authorities have been set up in several sectors to produce competitive outcomes, i.e. foster greater efficiency in resource allocation and consumer welfare through maintaining and promoting competition. The question of overlapping jurisdictions, between the competition authority and sectoral regulators, is going be a challenge and would require a proper mechanism to resolve the same.

RECOMMENDATIONS

- Adopt a National Competition Policy for the country, so that Government and the regulatory agencies are aware of, and take into account, the competition dimension in their own policy formulation and implementation
- Create awareness, among all stakeholders, about Competition Policy and Law, and other Regulatory Laws which promote competition in different sectors
- Support the consumer movement, with financial resources to enable the competition, and other regulatory authorities to perform advocacy roles
- Ensure independence of the Competition and Regulatory Authorities
- Create State-level competition and regulatory laws to resolve local problems

3

Competition Act, 2002: The Approach

S. CHAKRAVARTHY*

Introduction

India has had a competition law—the Monopolies & Restrictive Trade Practices Act (MRTPA) since 1969, which has been amended over time. The last amendment was done in 1991 to remove the licensing role of the MRTP Commission (MRTPC) and dilute the merger control provisions to adapt to economic reforms, which set in the same year. Though, over time, it was realised that markets need to be regulated—the type of problems which arose, could not be handled by the MRTPA. Following that, and through a consultative process, the Competition Act, 2002, (Act, for brief) was passed by the Parliament.

The distinctions between the MRTPA and the Act can be seen from Table 3.1.

The new competition law of India, namely, the Competition Act, 2002 in its preamble highlights the following major objectives:

- Prevent practices having adverse effect on competition
- Promote and sustain competition in the markets
- Protect the interests of consumers
- Ensure freedom of trade carried on by other participants in markets in India

The preamble also mandates that the economic development of the country needs to be kept in view, in implementing the objectives of

* Former Member, MRTP Commission, Adviser/Consultant on Competition Policy and Law, and Fellow, CUTS Centre for Competition, Investment & Economic Regulation (C-CIER).

the Act. The policy should be such that it supports the country's overall development path.

Table 3.1

S. No.	*MRTP Act, 1969*	*Competition Act, 2002*
1.	Based on pre-reforms command and control regime	Based on post-reforms liberalised regime
2.	Based on size/structure as factor	Based on conduct as a factor
3.	Competition offences implicit and not defined	Competition offences explicit and defined
4.	Complex in arrangement and language	Simple in arrangement and language, and comprehensible
5.	Frowns upon dominance	Frowns upon abuse of dominance
6.	Registration of agreements compulsory	No requirement of registration of agreements
7.	No combinations regulations (post-1991 amendment)	Combination regulations beyond a high threshold limit
8.	No competition advocacy role for the MRTPC	CCI has competition advocacy role
9.	No penalties for offences	Penalties for offences
10.	Reactive and rigid	Proactive and flexible
11.	Unfair trade practices covered	Unfair trade practices omitted (Consumer Protection Act, 1986 will deal with them)
12.	Rule of law approach	Rule of reason approach
13.	Blanket exclusion of intellectual property rights	Exclusion of intellectual property rights, but unreasonable restrictions covered

Highlights of The Act

The new Act essentially focuses on four core areas:

1) Anti-competitive Agreements

Firms enter into agreements, which have the potential of restricting competition. They could be formally written documents or oral understandings, and could be horizontal or vertical.

a) ***Horizontal Agreements***: Agreements between two or more enterprises that are at the same stage of the production chain, and in the same market, constitute the horizontal variety. The Act has taken care to define the relevant market. To attract the provisions of law, the products must be substitutable. The Act outlaws any agreement, which causes or is likely to cause an appreciable adverse effect on competition within India. The 'rule of reason' test is used for determining the illegality of an agreement, except in the four types listed in the following paragraph.

Four types of agreements between enterprises, involved in the same or similar manufacturing, or trading of goods or services, are presumed to have an appreciable adverse effect on competition and are therefore *per se* illegal:

- agreements regarding prices,
- agreements regarding quantities,
- agreements on bidding, and
- agreements to share or divide markets.

Horizontal agreements, which include cartels, are presumed to lead to unreasonable restrictions of competition and are, therefore, presumed to have an adverse effect on competition.

The Act contains *leniency provisions*, which provide for a reduced penalty on a participant in a cartel, who makes a full disclosure of having violated the Act. Be that as it may, the catch is, that the firm that spills the beans, should have done it before the prosecution started. In criminal cases, there is a similar provision, called approver, but the individual can seek leniency after being charge-sheeted also. The logic behind the leniency provisions is that a cartel is a hard nut to crack. This has been quite successful in the USA and has been adopted by other authorities, such as the European Commission also. More often than not, cartels do not have a formal or a written agreement.

b) ***Vertical Agreements***: Vertical agreements, in most competition regimes, are not subjected to the rigours of the law. However, where a vertical agreement has the character of distorting or preventing competition, it is not spared from the ambit of law. The Act lists certain factors, *inter alia,* to be taken into account to determine whether an agreement or a practice has an appreciable effect on competition. The factors are:

- creation of entry barriers in the market,
- driving existing competitors out of the market,

- accrual of benefits to consumers, and
- improvement in production or distribution of goods.

Exceptions

The Act, however, lays down two exceptions to the applicability of the provisions relating to anti-competitive agreements:

i) Intellectual Property Protection with Reasonable Conditions: The Act recognises that the bundle of rights that are subsumed in Intellectual Property Rights (IPR) should not be disturbed in the interests of creativity and intellectual/innovative power of the human mind. However, the relationship between competition law control and intellectual property rights is inherently contradictory, as there is a potential conflict between the two. This is because the existence and the exercise of intellectual property rights may generate anti-competitive effects through the monopoly power, granted to the holders of the rights.

The Act does not permit any *unreasonable condition* forming a part of protection or exploitation of intellectual property rights. Some unreasonable conditions that may accompany IPR licences and are likely to limit competition, and attract the provisions of the Act include:

- patent pooling,
- tie-in arrangements,
- prohibiting licensees to use competing technology,
- an agreement to continue paying royalty even after the patent has expired, and
- fixing the prices at which licensees should sell.

In many competition laws of the world, IPRs are excluded from the coverage. Anyhow, a European case law has said that the IPR *per se* is not violative of the competition law, but its abuse is certainly covered. The WTO Agreement TRIPS also requires governments to enact suitable legislation to cover the abuse of IPRs.

ii) Export Cartels: As is the case of most jurisdictions, export cartels are outside the purview of the Act. A justification of this exemption is that most countries do not desire any shackles in their export efforts, as the problem lies elsewhere.

2) *Abuse of Dominance*

A dominant position has been defined in the Act in terms of the 'position of strength' enjoyed by an enterprise in the relevant market in India, which enables it to operate independently of competitive forces prevailing in the relevant market; or to affect its competitors or consumers or the relevant market in its favour. There are two platforms to determine a relevant market—the product market and the geographical market.

The Act does not consider dominance as such as prejudicing competition. But it outlaws abuse of dominance. The actions that are considered anti-competitive and illegal in the context of agreements are also illegal, if undertaken by a dominant firm. These include charging or paying unfair prices; and restriction on quantities, markets and technical development. A greater threat to competition is from the actions of dominant firms that are inimical to future competition.

One such example is the practice of *Predatory Pricing*. This is one of the most pernicious forms of abuse of dominance. It occurs when an enterprise sells goods or provides services at a price, which is below the cost of producing the goods or providing the service, with a view to limiting competition or driving out competitors, and then raises prices to recoup its losses. Predation can be mainly established after the act, i.e. once the rival has left the market and the predator has acquired a monopoly position in the market. Before predatory pricing indictment is arrived at, it is necessary that the intent to eliminate the competitor or competition is established. If not, mere offer of a price lower than the cost of production will not automatically be indicted under the Act. The distinction between 'predatory pricing' and 'price competition' is often very grey and not easily ascertainable. In a few cases in the USA, Australia and Jamaica, the action against offending parties, on this ground, have failed.

3) *Combinations Regulation*

Combinations, in terms of the meaning given to them in the Act, include mergers, amalgamations, acquisitions and acquisitions of control, which are above a certain threshold. The thresholds are quite high and have been elaborated in the Act. For want of space, they are not defined here. During the debate on the draft

Competition Bill (before the Act was passed), there was a general feeling that Indian companies, being small, needed to combine to become active international players. Accordingly, the thresholds have been kept high.

Yet, combinations are a legitimate means by which firms can grow, and are as much a part of the organic process of industrial evolution and restructuring as new entry, growth and exit, but they may raise competition concerns. For instance, horizontal mergers have the potential for reducing competition and are generally the focus of attention. In rare cases, when an enterprise in a dominant position enters into a vertical merger with another firm in an adjacent market, to further entrench its position of dominance, it provides a clear cause for concern.

The Act has made the pre-notification of combinations voluntary for the parties concerned. Still, if the parties to the combination choose not to notify the Competition Commission of India (CCI), as it is not mandatory, they run the risk of a post-combination action by the CCI, if it is discovered, subsequently, that the combination has an appreciable adverse effect on competition. The Act has laid down a list of factors to be taken into account for the purpose of determining whether the combination would have an appreciable adverse effect on competition. The Mergers Bench of the CCI is mandated to adjudicate on mergers by weighing potential efficiency losses against potential gains. A caveat however merits mention here. It is easy to make an omelette out of an egg, but it is difficult to unscramble an omelette. It is not impossible, though, as was seen in some cases in the USA, such as the break up of AT&T.

4) Competition Advocacy

The purpose of competition advocacy is to create a culture of competition. The CCI is empowered to participate in the formulation of the country's economic policies, and to participate in reviewing the laws that impinge on competition at the instance of the Central Government. The catch in this is that the CCI can merely advocate to the Government only when called to do so, and its recommendations are advisory and not binding. Intelligent and innovative ways can be found by the CCI to raise its flag even without being called for by the Government. This can be done through well-researched discussion papers, like what the Telecom Regulatory Authority of India brings out.

The other advocacy function of the CCI is to do advocacy with the public at large, to create a better understanding of competition issues. In order to promote competition advocacy and create awareness about competition issues, and also to accord training to all concerned, the Act enjoins the establishment of a fund christened the *Competition Fund*.

Other Important Features of The Act

Investigation, Prosecution and Adjudication

The adjudicative wing is distinct from the investigative wing in the Act. At the apex of the investigative wing is the Director General (DG), who will only look into the complaints received from the CCI and submit the findings to it. The DG does not have *suo motu* powers of investigation and the investigators will solely be making inquiries at the instance of the CCI. Under the Act, the DG is also the prosecuting authority.

The Act deviates from the earlier tradition of appointing only bureaucrats in the investigation team, as under the MRTP Act, and instead seeks to bring in professionals like economists, lawyers, accountants, etc, as investigators. The Act thus induces professionalism in the investigative arm – a step in the right direction.

CCI, with autonomy and administrative powers, is the adjudicating body under the Act. The Act provides for a separate Merger Bench, which is a part of the CCI.

To ensure competent and effective implementation of competition policy and competition law, it is important and imperative to select suitable individuals and free the CCI of any Government control. While it is practically difficult to eliminate political favouritism in appointments, it can be minimised, to a great extent, by resorting to a *collegium selection process*. The Government has opted for a search committee procedure for the selection of a Chairperson and Members. A writ petition before the Supreme Court has, *inter alia,* challenged the appointment of a retired bureaucrat as the Chairperson, and has sought the appointment of a retired judge to that post. The matter is *sub judice*.

Independence of CCI

There are certain provisions in the Act, which undermine the independence and autonomy of the CCI. These include prior approval of the Government, required by the Chairperson, in the matter of transfer of a Member from one Bench, situated in one city, to another Bench, situated in another city and the granting of money at the Government's discretion, etc. CCI is also bound by directions of the Government on questions of policy, and the power given to the Government to supersede the CCI on grounds of public interest, for example. There is also a draconian provision under which the Government can remove members of the CCI, under four grounds, quite easily. These provisions, which impact on the independence and autonomy of the CCI, require another look and appropriate amendments.

Appeals and Review Provisions

Appeals against the decisions and orders of the CCI rest with the Supreme Court within the limitation period of 60 days. Hence, the status given to the CCI is very high, with only the Supreme Court having the power to overturn its orders.

This may change in the future, as in the matter of the writ petition pending before the Supreme Court—the Government had indicated its thinking in favour of an appellate authority, to hear appeals against the CCI's orders. As with most adjudicatory bodies, the CCI has the power to review its own order on an application made by the aggrieved party.

Phased Introduction of The Act

The Government has decided on a calibrated introduction of the Act, i.e. the four main sections will be introduced in a phased manner. During the first year of the introduction of this Act, the MRTPA would be operational concurrently, as the CCI would be engaged in competition advocacy functions only.

During the second year, the provisions relating to Anti-competitive Agreements and Abuse of Dominance would be brought into force. The MRTP Act would then stand repealed, and the MRTP Commission wound up. During the third year, provisions relating to Combinations Regulation would be brought into force. This calibrated introduction of the Act is strategically a step in the right direction, as it will help the country to progress gradually, but steadily and surely, on competition related matters.

Extraterritorial Jurisdiction

The Act has extraterritorial reach. This provision is based on what is known as the *'effects doctrine'*. This implies that if an action or practice is outside the shores of India, but has an appreciable adverse effect on competition in the relevant market in India, it can be brought within the ambit of the Act.

Concerns

Despite the above-mentioned, progressive features of the Act, various concerns have been raised on the following aspects:

Combinations Regulation

Concerns have been expressed, especially from the business lobby, that a merger control regime will hinder the growth of Indian businesses, which are required to face foreign competition in a global environment.

A response to this is that the Act does not intend to discourage mergers and other combinations, unless they are anti-competitive in nature or detrimental to the interest of the consumers. Matters have to be decided on the *rule of reason* basis.

Accountability of CCI

It is apprehended that the CCI will be a new monster, and that the corporate sector will have to bow down to one more "controller" in the country.

It needs to be emphasised that the Act is not another law, supplementing the existing MRTPA. This law succeeds and supplants the outgoing MRTPA. The new law is simpler, flexible and more liberal than the MRTPA. In order to allay this fear, the CCI should be made accountable, through independent review by consumer organisations, external agencies, and peer review by competition authorities from other countries. In case of South Africa, the OECD Global Forum on Competition assessed the country's competition policy institutions.

Unfair Trade Practices Not a Part of the Act

The MRTPA deals with unfair trade practices, and there is significant overlap with the Consumer Protection Act, 1986 (COPRA), on the provisions relating to 'unfair trade practices'. Because of this, the new law does not contain provisions relating to unfair trade practices, as they are covered *in extenso* in COPRA. With provisions on unfair trade practices removed, the CCI may face a major challenge to get the public buy-in, and to create a public image. But it needs to be underscored that deletion of the provisions relating to 'unfair trade practices' was triggered by the need to avoid the overlap mentioned above.

Therefore, even with the handicap, the CCI should take up consumers' issues, which are of systemic nature, to create a public buy-in. These could include: tied sales in schools and colleges, over uniforms and stationery; or the tie-up of doctors with diagnostic clinics (see chapter on Competition Abuses at Consumer Level).

RECOMMENDATIONS

- Make the Competition Commission of India (CCI) independent of Government funding and control
- Establish coordination mechanisms between the CCI and other agencies on common issues concerning market abuse
- CCI should take up systemic issues that directly affect consumers, to create a public buy-in
- Enable a high level of professionalism through proactive efforts and benchmarks
- Provide regular training exposure for capacity building of staff
- Competition Commission should examine cases taken up under the MRTP Act, in particular the significant ones which failed, and prepare a compendium of case laws
- Independent review of CCI should be built-in, to ensure its accountability

4

Mergers and Acquisitions in India: Implications for Competition

MANISH AGARWAL*

Introduction

'Merger or Amalgamation' is defined as a combination of two companies wherein at least one loses its corporate existence. The surviving company, also called the merged company, acquires both the assets and liabilities of the company that loses its existence. *'Acquisition or Takeover,'* on the other hand, means acquisition of a certain block of equity capital of a company, which enables the acquirer to exercise control over the affairs of the company thus acquired. In India, a holding of 26 per cent of equity of a company makes the holder a strategic partner, and leads to the exercise of effective control.

In terms of markets involved, mergers and acquisitions (M&As) are classified as:

- *Horizontal,* where both firms are in the same product market. The merger of the two pharmaceutical companies, Glaxo and Smithkline Beecham, is one such example.
- *Vertical* merger is between firms engaged in different stages of the production cycle. An example of a vertical merger is the merger of Uptron Colour Picture Tubes Ltd. (manufacturer of picture tubes used in colour television sets) with BPL Ltd (a manufacturer of electronics, including colour television sets).
- *Conglomerate* mergers are those mergers, which are neither horizontal nor vertical. For example, the merger of Global

* Policy Analyst, CUTS Centre for Competition, Investment & Economic Regulation (C-CIER)

Sugars (manufacturer of sugar) with Kitply Industries (manufacturer of wood products).

M&As from Competition Policy Perspective

Firms resort to M&As for a variety of reasons—to realise economies of scale, expansion and growth, and improve operating performance. While these motives are desirable, concerns arise when mergers lead to increased market power wielded by the merged entity. This is most obvious in the case of horizontal mergers, as they provide the clearest example of possible anticompetitive effects. The reason is that any such merger reduces the number of competitors, and therefore raises the possibility of creating dominance in the market.

Vertical mergers can have similar potential effects, as vertical integration, combined with substantial market power at one level, may permit an extension of that market power to the other level. For example, if a firm has a monopoly over the supply of a particular input and it integrates downstream into processing of the input into a finished product. An anticompetitive effect may arise if the firm charges a high price for the input supplies and a low price for the finished product. This differential price jeopardises the economic viability of all the other firms in the downstream finished product market. This practice is prevalent in the steel industry, where integrated steel manufacturers follow differential pricing in hot-rolled coils to harm the interests of cold-rolled steel manufacturers, the downstream players (See chapter on the Steel Industry).

By and large, conglomerate mergers may not have the potential for reducing competition and are generally beyond the purview of any law on mergers.

In effect, a merger leads to a 'bad' outcome only if it creates a dominant enterprise that subsequently abuses its dominance. To some extent, the issue overlaps with the issue of dominance and its abuse. Viewed in this way, there is probably no need to have provisions for merger control in competition law. The reason, that such a provision exists in most laws, is to pre-empt the potential abuse of dominance where it is probable, as subsequent unbundling can be both difficult and socially costly.

M&As in India

The liberalised regime followed since the early 1990s has increased the possibility of industrial restructuring and consolidation through M&As by removing restrictions under the Industrial Licensing Policy, Foreign Exchange Regulation Act (FERA), and the Capital Issues Control Act. Besides, major amendments were made to the Monopolies and Restrictive Trade Practices Act (MRTPA) in 1991, by which the provisions on mergers and acquisitions were removed. Consequently, there has been a spurt in merger activity since the early 90's (Figure 4.1). A high level of merger activity is observed, in particular since 1995-96, with each subsequent year recording more than 100 deals.

FIGURE 4.1

Number of Mergers (1973-74 to 2002-03)

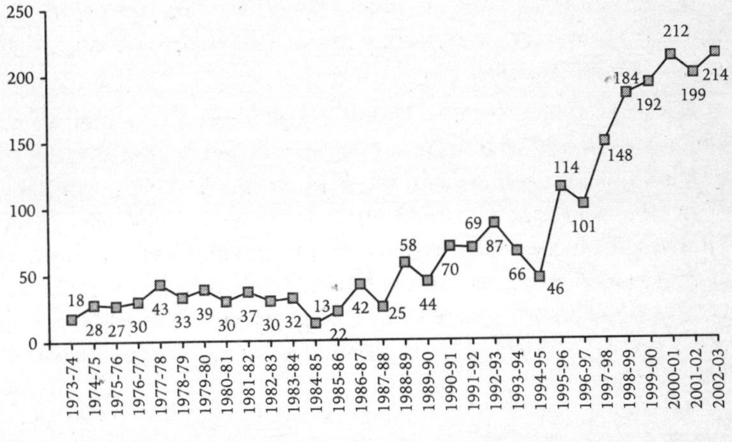

Source: Research & Statistics Division, Department of Company Affairs.

In general, horizontal type of combinations have been the main form of M&A in India, suggesting that firms have been trying to consolidate in the same product market. What is more, in a significant number of cases, both the companies belong to the same business group. In terms of industries, M&As during the 90s have been largely concentrated in electrical machinery, electronics, textiles, drugs & pharmaceuticals, iron & steel, beverages, financial services, and computer software.

Be that as it may, not much work has been done to analyse the impact of M&As on performance of firms and market power. On the other hand, the little work that has been done shows that, in general, performance of merged firms did not improve. Furthermore, there has been an increase in concentration in industries, where there is a higher incidence of M&As.

Given the liberalised policy framework, in particular, the liberal attitude towards FDI inflows, transnational corporations (TNCs) have increasingly used the M&A route to enter and strengthen their presence in the country. The bulk of deals relating to TNCs have taken place since 1996 and have mostly involved acquisitions rather than mergers. An increasing proportion of TNC related M&As is found in the field of services, where they are seeking to establish a place of business in the country, by acquiring established domestic enterprises and their networks. The deals involving TNCs are predominantly horizontal in nature. Among others, the primary motives are to enter the Indian market and extend the scope of operations, or the consolidation of market share.

It has been observed that certain mergers relating to foreign firms involved market shares of a magnitude that would attract the attention of competition authorities in most countries, but in India, all merger and acquisition activities were beyond challenge. Thus, although the merger of Lipton and Brooke Bond into Hindustan Lever Limited parent Unilever passed unchallenged in India, the Pakistan competition authority succeeded in getting Unilever to withdraw one of its brands, and reduce its shareholding in Brooke Bond Pakistan to 40 per cent[1]!

M&A Regulation in India

Monopolies and Restrictive Trade Practices Act, 1969

Under the Act, MRTP companies[2] were required to seek Central Government's approval to undertake a merger or acquisition. These

1. Bhattacharjea, Aditya, "Trade, Investment, and Competition Policy: An Indian Perspective," in Aaditya Mattoo and Robert M. Stern ed., *India and the WTO*, 2003
2. Companies were classified as MRTP companies if they had asset value of at least Rs. 100 crore (raised from Rs. 20 crore during the 1985 amendments) or were dominant in the relevant market, commanding a market share in excess of one-fourth

provisions gave absolute power to the Central Government in matters relating to M&As involving MRTP companies.

The restrictions remained in vogue for over two decades, until the 1991 amendments to the Act, when provisions relating to pre-entry restrictions for any expansion, new investment or M&A activities involving MRTP companies, were all deleted from the statute. The scrapping of pre-entry restrictions was expected to encourage competition by reducing barriers to entry for new firms, and to enable Indian firms to become large enough to compete effectively in global markets. With the amendments, size as a factor to discourage concentration of economic power, was given up and focus shifted to curbing monopolistic, restrictive and unfair trade practices.

The amendments had a significant impact on the merger behaviour of MRTP companies, as most of these firms acquired another firm that belonged to the same management and/or produced a similar product (Table 4.1). It can be argued that these firms could not have opted for this route of expansion if the government had not diluted the MRTPA.

Table 4.1

Merger Behaviour of MRTP Cos. (pre- & post-1991 amendments)

	5 years pre-91 (1986-87 to 1990-91)	*5 years post-91 (1992-93 to 1996-97)*
% of mergers where both companies belong to the same business group	17% (13 out of 77)	63% (60 out of 96)
% of mergers where both companies belong to the same product category	38% (22 out of 58)	53% (48 out of 90)

Competition Act, 2002

The Competition Act, 2002, is set to replace the MRTP Act. The Act has provisions for regulations of 'combinations', which include mergers, amalgamations, and acquisitions, beyond a specified threshold limit. The threshold limit is Rs. 1,000 crore (US$208 mn, on 2004 exchange rate) in terms of aggregate value of assets, of the combining parties, or Rs.3,000 crore (US$625 mn) in terms of turnover of the combining parties. In the event either or both of the parties are outside India, the threshold is US$500 mn for assets and US$1500 mn for turnover. If one of the merging parties belongs to a group, which controls it, the threshold is Rs.4,000 crore (US$833 mn) in terms of assets and Rs.12,000 crore (US$2.5 bn) in terms of turnover. If the group has assets or turnover outside India also, the threshold limits are US$2.0 bn for assets and US$6.0 bn for turnover.

HLL-TOMCO Merger Case (post-1991 amendments)

The first controversial merger, post-1991 amendments, that did not have to pass the acid test of the MRTP Commission, was between Hindustan Lever Limited (HLL) and Tata Oil Mills Company Ltd. (TOMCO), both significant players in the market for soaps and detergents.

The merger was challenged on various grounds by the HLL employees' union. One of the arguments was that the merger would result in a large share of the market being controlled by a multinational company, and that consumer interests might be adversely affected. However, the Supreme Court held that the merger could not be stopped on the grounds that it violated public interest or public policy. The judgement held that the MRTP and FERA amendments were specifically intended to allow foreign firms to do business in India more easily, and what has been expressly authorised by the statute cannot be struck down as being against the public policy.

The Court opined that consumer interests could be considered, if after the merger it is found that the merged entity is working in a way, which brings it within the purview of the MRTP Act. Under such circumstances, the MRTP Commission can take any action as it deems fit. Nevertheless, the concern is that section 27 of MRTPA, which empowers the government to order division of an undertaking or sever interconnections between undertakings, has never been used.

Market share data compiled by the Centre for Monitoring Indian Economy (CMIE, 1999) shows that HLL's market share in soaps rose from 19.7 per cent in 1992-93 (the year before the merger with TOMCO) to 26 per cent in 1997-98; in synthetic detergents it rose from 33.1 per cent to 46.7 per cent. Market research data (Naidu 2000) put its share of toilet soaps and shampoos at over 60 per cent and detergent bars at 45 per cent.

Source: Bhattacharjea, Aditya, "Trade, Investment, and Competition Policy: An Indian Perspective," in Aaditya Mattoo and Robert M. Stern ed., *India and the WTO*, 2003

The threshold limits are subject to revision every two years on the basis of wholesale price index, or fluctuations in exchange rate of rupee or foreign currencies. These limits are prescribed in such a way that, by and large, only major mergers and acquisitions would fall within the ambit of the Act. Around 13 criteria have been built in, to determine the adverse effects of a combination on competition.

The Act makes it voluntary for the companies concerned to notify their proposed combination to the Mergers Bench (a part of the Competition Commission of India), though the Draft Bill that preceded the Act had mandatory notification provisions. The initial proposal for mandatory review of proposed mergers faced tremendous criticism from business lobbies, and was diluted by making pre-merger notification voluntary. Even the threshold limit was doubled due to business opposition. The trigger cause for these changes was that companies in India needed to grow in size, in order to become globally competitive.

The Merger Bench of the CCI is mandated to adjudicate on combinations by weighing potential efficiency losses against potential gains. As per the provisions in the Act, approval is automatically granted if no decision is reached in 90 days. On the other hand, the Act empowers the CCI to look into a combination *up to a year after it has taken effect* and to undo or modify it, if the combination causes, or is likely to cause, an appreciable adverse effect on competition within the relevant markets in India. But, ordering a demerger tantamounts to the unscrambling of an omelette and could be a costly affair, requiring technical expertise in the Commission. A similar provision existed in the MRTPA, but no case for demerger ever came up before it.

In comparison, in the USA, demergers have been carried out successfully in the past, such as the mini-Bells case, where AT&T, the giant telecom company, was broken up into seven companies in 1984, in response to a federal anti-trust suit. Currently, the trend is not against big mergers.

There are two concerns that arise relating to M&As under the Competition Act. *First*, the expression 'combination' as defined in the Act is very narrow in scope, as it leaves out those mergers and acquisitions, which fall below the threshold limits, but may cause an appreciable adverse effect on competition. This is likely in cases where the overall market size is small, or the merger involves a product whose relevant market is local/regional in nature.

One such instance could be merger/acquisition between companies in the cement industry. The cement industry is of a regional nature, given that freight costs are a significant proportion of the final cost of cement. Given that the formation of a cartel is *per se* illegal, companies in the cement industry that want to indulge in anti-competitive activities in a region will most likely resort to a merger or acquisition, as it would be relatively easy to carry out, given the high threshold limits specified in the Act. (See chapter on Cement). As a consequence, any merger/acquisition among the top companies in a region might raise competition concerns, but would be out of the ambit of the Competition Act, because of high threshold limits.

Second, the Act mentions that the CCI shall not initiate an inquiry into a combination after the expiry of one year from the date on which the combination has taken effect. Nonetheless, the effective date of merger is not specified in the Act, which is normally the date on which assets and liabilities of the target company get vested in the acquirer company. It is observed that in most merger cases, the effective date precedes the date on which the merger order is passed, by the high court concerned. Given this, would the CCI initiate an inquiry, when companies file their application with the high court or, after the high court has passed an order?

In the former case, the CCI has to inform the high court of the inquiry it has initiated, and coordinate with the court in conducting the inquiry. In the latter case, the CCI may not even get time to conduct an inquiry, if it takes the effective date of merger as defined above. This is because in several cases, a high court often takes a year to arrive at its decision. Even if the high court takes less than a year, the CCI would effectively have only a few months to conduct and complete the investigation. This issue needs to be taken care of, when Statutory Regulations are framed.

Other Acts and Regulations

M&As are covered by the Companies Act, 1956. In case of mergers, high court's approval is required, which examines the application with a view to *protect the interests of creditors and shareholders*. For acquisitions, prior approval of the Central Government is required. A time period of 60 days is given to refuse to grant such approvals, otherwise the approval is presumed to have been granted. The Central government's decision is based on the grounds of *protecting the interests of the target company and public interest*.

Acquisition of listed companies are also governed by the Securities and Exchange Board of India's (SEBI) Takeover Code, which provides for transparency, relating to the acquisition of shares of listed companies, and is designed to *protect shareholders' interests*. In particular, the Code has been designed to protect companies from hostile takeovers.

M&A is also covered under certain sectoral acts/regulations, such as in Electricity, Banking and Telecommunications. As per the Electricity Act, 2003, the appropriate regulatory commission (federal level or state level) considers the criteria of *public interest* to grant approval. In Banking, the Reserve Bank of India has been regulating M&As, among private sector banks, to ensure that it is in *depositors' interest and public interest*.

In Telecommunications, following the recommendations of the Telecom Regulatory Authority of India (TRAI) on intra-circle mergers and acquisitions, the Department of Telecommunications (DoT) has framed its guidelines. In order to ensure that *sufficient competition exists*, intra-circle merger/acquisition is allowed, subject to the condition that, post-merger, there were at least three operators within the telecom circle for that service, and the market share of the merged entity in that service area does not exceed 67 per cent.

Thus, except for the DoT guidelines, which take into account competition concerns, M&A provisions in other Acts/Regulations do not regulate M&As from the competition perspective. Accordingly, after the 1991 amendment, and with the exception of the DoT guidelines, there is at present no regulation of M&As in India from the competition angle. The provisions relating to combination regulations in the Competition Act would be brought into force during the third year of the operation of the Act. But even this will leave out certain M&As, which may pose competition concerns.

National Champions

The Finance Ministry is exploring the issue of merging the country's public sector banks to create a few mammoth banks. There is also a move to create a massive development financial institution

(DFI) by merging all existing DFIs. The purpose is to create giant, Indian financial entities that can take on competition in the global market. Similarly, the Petroleum Ministry is exploring options of merging companies in the oil sector, to create oil behemoths, that have financial capabilities to match firms in the international market.

Yet, there are both pros and cons to creating national champions.

Pros...	*... and Cons*
· Economies of scale	· Abuse of dominance
· International competitiveness	· Anti-competitive behaviour
· R&D promotion	· Reduction of competition in relevant markets
· Spillover effects to stimulate other industries and economic development of home country	· Consumer interest concerns
· National security grounds	· Possible distortions to FDI, trade flows and friction among trading partners
· Dynamic growth and development	· Possible misuse by special interest groups

In the UK and The Netherlands, Government intervention into the enforcement of competition policy, in regulating mergers and acquisitions with regard to "national interests", is limited to national security grounds at most. But, in countries like Germany, Canada and Australia, the "national champion" argument has considerable significance.

The experiences with pro-'national champions' industrial policy in certain countries illustrate the benefits that can be derived by helping domestic firms become more efficient and competitive. For example, the success of the Korean industrialisation programme relied on a big business-oriented growth strategy, together with regulations on entry and protection from foreign competition.

In Korea, the government helped create giant corporations, the *Chaebol*, which went on to capture the world markets. Importantly, the giant Korean *chaebols* were made to compete with each other for government support. Still, the *chaebol*-led economic growth eventually took its toll on the Korean economy. The market structure became distorted due to the existence of monopolistic practices, leading to a strong public outcry in the 1980s.

Recognising the need to remedy such distortion, the Korean Government enacted the Monopoly Regulation and Fair Trade Act in 1980, and established the Korea Fair Trade Commission (FTC) in 1981. The matter of competition has been treated very seriously by Korea, as the head of the FTC is a member of the cabinet. This enables the competition authority to have its say in most economic policy matters.

The challenge is to strike the right balance, so that the pursuit of national development strategy is not misused by special interest groups and wrong 'winners' picked, proving detrimental to competition and consumer welfare.

If size were of essence in global competitiveness, then State Bank of India (SBI) and Industrial Development Bank of India (IDBI) would have been exporters of financial services.[3] The path to globally competitive finance does not lie in bigger Public Sector Unit (PSU) banks, but in asking questions about why Bank of Baroda and IDBI are so far behind the well-run banks of India. If a Dena Bank is merged into IDBI, we will not get a globally competitive bank. We will just get a bigger IDBI.

Another aspect to consider is that when a PSU becomes large there are unique sets of problems that arise. Being so big, no government could accept bankruptcy. The threat of bankruptcy is a central device through which a firm is kept honest. A policy of mergers will diminish this pressure on the PSUs and detract them from efficiency. In a 1998 merger case involving the four largest banks in Canada, the country's Finance Ministry rejected the merger proposals. One of the grounds for rejecting the merger proposals was the fear of reduced policy flexibility for the Government to address potential, future prudential concerns, as allowing two banks to operate will sharply increase the overall systemic risk in case one of them failed.

In the context of the oil sector, a discussion paper brought out by the Ministry of Petroleum and Natural Gas highlights that the PSU oil companies under-performed against their private sector rivals, in core businesses. The higher profitability of PSUs came mostly from the dismantling of the administered pricing mechanism (resulting in cartelised pricing), lack of competition, and higher international oil prices.

3. Patnaik, Ila, "PSU Mergers: Are Bigger Things Better?" *Financial Express*, November 22, 2004

Be that as it may, in oil, big is truly beautiful and captivating. The world over, vertically integrated oil and gas businesses are the norm. The merger of Chevron and Texaco, or that of Exxon and Mobil are two such examples. The oil and gas business is highly capital-intensive and requires serious risk-taking, in exploration, calling for deep pockets. The standard practice is to foray downstream, into retail sales of petroleum products to garner volumes. Anyhow, in the Indian public sector, the exploration and production major, ONGC, was restricted to the upstream; and the refining and retailing major, IOC, was confined to the downstream.

An important aspect to consider, is that of competition in the two sectors. Both banking and oil suffer from a lack of competition. It is imperative for the Government to create an open market, and a level playing field, to encourage competition for the companies to reach global standards of performance. The interests of the citizen will be ill-served by more concentrated banking or a more concentrated oil industry. It is important to ensure that the market process is acknowledged to realise the benefits from promoting national champions.

RECOMMENDATIONS

- Competition Commission should also monitor those M&As, which are out of the ambit of the Competition Act but may raise competition concerns
- Proper coordination is required between the Competition Commission and other agencies that regulate M&As (i.e. sectoral regulators, RBI, SEBI, High Court, etc)
- To realise the benefits from promoting national champions, it is important to ensure that the market process is acknowledged
- Public interest is an important factor in approving a merger or acquisition proposal. Care should be taken to ensure that it is not misused by special interest groups at the cost of consumer welfare
- The country has witnessed a tremendous spurt in M&As ever since economic reforms were initiated. An impact analysis of M&As should be conducted in terms of efficiency gains and market power

5

Cross-Border Competition Issues

ADITYA BHATTACHARJEA*
NITYA NANDA#

Introduction

As countries integrate more and more into the global economy, they become more prone to the anti-competitive practices operating on a global scale, or originating elsewhere in the world. India is no exception to this. When competition authorities from highly developed countries/blocks like the European Union face difficulties in handling cases with a cross-border dimension, it is clear that the authorities in developing countries face even greater and more serious problems.

Before we look further into the issue of tackling cross-border anti-competitive practices, let us briefly look into the various types of such practices that affect countries. These can broadly be classified into four groups:

- Market power in global or export markets;
- Barriers to import competition;
- Foreign investment; and
- Intellectual property rights

Cross-border Market Power

International Cartels

International cartels have attracted much attention in recent years. Competition (anti-trust) agencies in the European Union and the United States have successfully prosecuted over 40 such cartels that

* Reader, Department of Economics, Delhi School of Economics, University of Delhi, Delhi

Policy Analyst, CUTS Centre for Competition, Investment & Economic Regulation (C-CIER)

operated in their jurisdictions during the 1990s, and slapped heavy fines on several companies. A World Bank study put the volume of developing countries' imports of just 19 of these cartel-affected products in 1997 at US$59.9 bn, representing 4.4 per cent of their total imports and 0.9 per cent of their GDP in that year. Another estimate shows that the vitamins cartel alone cost developing countries US$3 bn during the 1990s.

Export Cartels

Most countries exempt export cartels from their antitrust laws, as long as they do not have any anti-competitive effect on the domestic market. In India, similar exception exist in both the outgoing MRTP Act and the new Competition Act.

Mergers and Acquisitions with Cross-border Dimensions

During the 1990s, there was a wave of mega-mergers, with firms merging with or acquiring controlling stakes in, other firms, often in other countries. Large companies merge in the developed world, and consequently, their subsidiaries and associates in developing countries too end up in new combinations. Moreover, developing countries may also be affected by merger and acquisition (M&A) activities that take place outside their territory, without any local presence.

Developing countries, to our knowledge, have dealt only with the first type of cases, i.e., subsidiaries merging as a result of a merger between parent companies internationally. But, even stopping the subsidiaries from merging would not serve any purpose, as both will continue to be controlled by the same parent company. Even if its competition law embodies the 'effects doctrine', a developing country will find it very difficult to enforce any such action against offshore mergers. Similar actions are, however, quite common in the developed world, based on the effects doctrine.

Cross-border Predatory Pricing

Cross-border predatory pricing can also lead to market distortions. Due to some striking similarities, cross-border predatory pricing is very often equated with dumping and thus, action is taken under anti-dumping legislation. Nevertheless, the principle underlying anti-dumping is different from that underlying competition law, in that it seeks to protect competitors and not competition. Though, in most developing countries, due to the small size of markets and low levels of market contestability, there would be more convergence between anti-dumping and anti-predation actions. Ironically, until recently, the main users of anti-dumping laws were developed countries. On the other hand, increasingly, developing countries too are taking recourse to these laws.

Barriers to Import Competition

Import cartels, vertical market restraints creating import barriers, private standard setting activities, abuse of monopsonistic dominance (dominance by one or few buyers) etc., may fall under this category.

Import cartels formed by domestic importers, or buyers and similar arrangements (such as boycotts of, or collective refusals to deal with, foreign competitors), may be a threat to maintaining competition in a market. In principle, a national competition law may generally be able to tackle such market-access barriers to foreign supplies and suppliers. Import cartels, whose function is solely to attempt to exercise monopsony power, in order to get a better price from foreign suppliers, may be viewed more favourably from a national efficiency and welfare perspective, than such cartels which exercise market power domestically. But, it may be difficult to make such a distinction or to separate the two types of activities.

Another way local firms gang up against foreign competitors is by preventing or hindering market access. For example, local firms will lobby their governments to disallow foreign manufacturers from marketing their goods. Other examples are when local firms lobby their governments to, either initiate unfair anti-dumping action or, raise import tariffs against foreign suppliers.

Foreign Investment

Foreign direct investment may increase competition in local markets, particularly in the investments of greenfield type. However, there is a possibility that takeovers of domestic firms may make the markets increasingly concentrated, to the extent of having one or a small number of dominant players. Moreover, even though a single instance of cross-border acquisition may seem to have no effect on competition, from a narrow national-market perspective, it may lead to a lessening of effective competition in the market, if the acquirer has been a major exporter to the country. Such acquisitions may be aimed at regional or global consolidation by TNCs.

In most developing countries, it has been seen that majority of the FDI comes in through acquisitions, rather than through fresh greenfield investments.

Intellectual Property Rights

Intellectual Property Rights (IPRs) may generate or contribute towards a position of market power. The IP holders typically engage in licensing arrangements with firms in different countries. The territorial nature of property rights, in such agreements, means that frequently the national law enables them to be used by rights holders to prevent parallel imports. In many cases, it has also been observed that cartels were built around patent cross-licensing schemes and thereby foreclosed competition.

The Indian Experience

International Cartels

According to one sanguine estimate, the vitamins cartel alone cost India about US$25 mn in the 1990s, due to overcharging. Country-specific estimates of losses are not available for other cartels. Some other important cartels that hit India very hard are those in heavy electrical equipments and flat rolled steel products. The operation of the international cartel on heavy electrical equipment, under the auspices of the International Electrical Association (involving most of the North American, European, some East European and Japanese firms), applied to all procurement outside of the EC and the US. India was one of the countries adversely affected by the conspiracy.

An international cartel on flat rolled steel products (which was in existence at least until the end 1994, and may still exist) with participation of European, Korean and Japanese firms, that divided the world (other than the US) with the area west of Myanmar coming under the sphere of European suppliers, and the area to the east under Korean and Japanese. This brought steel importers from Thailand, Indonesia, Malaysia or the Philippines under the influence of Japanese mills. Meanwhile India, a large importer of hot-rolled flat steel, could only import small amounts from Japan, since it was under the sphere of European mills. India has significant production capacity in some of the products, but its producers were not part of the global cartel and they were sufficiently punished for that, especially at the time of global recession in the sector.

Foreign Export Cartels and Predatory Pricing

The Indian MRTP Commission was unable to take any action against any of the international cartels that attracted the attention of other competition authorities for over-pricing. It did, nonetheless, respond to complaints by two Indian manufacturers' associations, against groups of foreign companies who had been selling at low prices, but these orders were set aside by the Supreme Court. The consequences of this ruling have informed the new Competition Act, which is designed to replace the MRTP Act, and is further discussed below.

Private Barriers in Foreign Markets

Evidence concerning India in this area is not well documented. Anyhow, a couple of examples may be worth mentioning. It may be noted that the Swiss Watch Manufacturers Association prevented the Indian watch manufacturer, Titan, from exhibiting their products at the Basel Jewellery and Watch Fair in Switzerland, using the pretext of the prevailing quantitative restrictions in India, which did not allow them to export to India. Similarly, Indian traders were not allowed to participate in the Dutch Flower Auctions.

Anti-dumping

The reduction of orthodox trade barriers has been accompanied by a proliferation of anti-dumping (AD) measures, in situations that could not possibly have been predatory pricing. The traditional users of AD have been the developed countries, particularly the US, the EU, and Canada. Indian exports, in the engineering and textiles sectors, have been repeatedly targeted by these countries, as well as by South Africa. But in recent years, developing countries have themselves become major users, with India now heading the list.

Cross-Border Issues in the Competition Act, 2002

The new Competition Act is yet to take effect at the time of writing. Be that as it may, some of its provisions relating to cross-border issues deserve comment. Section 3(5)(ii) states that "nothing in this section [on anti-competitive agreements] shall restrict ... the right of any person to export goods from India to the extent to which the agreement relates exclusively to the production, supply, distribution or control of goods or provision of services for such export". Section 32 states that, notwithstanding any restrictive agreement, any party to such agreement, any enterprise abusing a dominant position, or any combination or party to combination outside India, the Competition Commission has the power to inquire into it, if it has an anti-competitive effect within the relevant market in India. This clearly re-states the effects doctrine, which should undo the Supreme Court's disabling of the MRTP Commission in that respect.

Sub-section 33(2) of the Act goes to the other extreme in undoing the effects of the Supreme Court's ruling. It allows the Competition Commission to grant a temporary injunction restraining any party from importing goods, if it can be established that such imports would contravene the Act's substantive provisions. If the foreign anti-competitive practice is indulged in by a cartel, then this measure would only make a bad situation worse by further restricting competition. If it is predatory pricing, then an import restriction might be reasonable. But a WTO Dispute Settlement ruling of 2000 held, in respect of the United States, that low-valued imports could only be tackled through anti-dumping remedies. Any other trade restriction would attract dispute settlement and retaliation by other WTO members.

The new Competition Commission, staffed at present by a handful of civil servants, will have to be equipped with the necessary resources, but the required expertise is scarce in India. Instead, multinational companies, who usually have highly skilled staff and consultants, with the requisite experience of fighting antitrust cases in countries where such criteria have been used for many years, will have a decisive advantage. Inexperienced Indian firms might bear the brunt of enforcement, while foreign firms get away with similar violations.

The Way Forward

In order to face the cross-border competition challenges, a well-functioning, national competition regime may be necessary but not sufficient. Developing country competition authorities, in general, do not have the resources or the experience to tackle international competition challenges. The provision of extra-territorial jurisdiction in a national competition law will have a very limited capability, if at all, especially in developing countries.

Some countries have entered into bilateral or regional agreements to deal with such problems. Competition provisions can be found in many of the bilateral trade agreements. Yet, in such agreements, the focus is on the market access issue, and hence, the competition provisions are not comprehensive enough to deal with the wide range of competition issues.

For political economy reasons as well, a regional approach is easier to sell. However, regional competition regimes will only focus on those cases in which anti-competitive practices have a regional dimension. Needless to say that bilateral agreements will have very limited impact. As a consequence, they can be best dealt with in a multilateral framework, rather than on a bilateral or regional basis.

The global community has been discussing the issue of a possible international framework on competition since the days of the Havana Charter, in the late 1940s. The discussions got a significant boost after the issue was introduced in the WTO agenda, during its Ministerial Conference in Singapore, in 1996. Even so the proposal for a competition agreement at the WTO played the role of one of the spoilsports at the 2003 Ministerial meeting at Cancun, and has now been formally dropped from the negotiating agenda. There is, by and large, an overall consensus that there is a case for a multilateral competition framework, but there is no agreement as to:

- What should be its scope and contours? and
- Where should it be institutionally situated?

Apart from UNCTAD and the WTO, the issue has been discussed at the OECD, which has a Standing Committee on Competition Policy and Law. The competition authorities of different countries have come together to promote the International Competition network (ICN).

Considering the present geo-political situation, it is highly unlikely that a consensus could emerge on a competition agreement at the WTO. Still, the consumers (and many producers too) would continue to pay for the anti-competitive practices operating at the global level. Accordingly, there is a feeling that other forums or initiatives, to promote international co-operation on competition, should be strengthened or launched, instead of pushing for a competition agreement at the WTO.

Developing countries, including India, would find it difficult to commit to an agreement on competition at the WTO, unless they are convinced of its benefits. Consequently, the best way forward in this regard, would be to evolve a competition framework at a non-controversial forum. A limited agreement on competition, involving market access issues, may be negotiated, but only at a later date when there is an "explicit consensus". Nonetheless, the bottom line is that it should be done, only if there is positive willingness and understanding among all members and, not through pressure tactics.

RECOMMENDATIONS

- Extra-territorial jurisdiction in the Competition Act, (2002) is a right step, but to make it effective—the Competition Commission of India would require substantial capacity building, and cooperation arrangements with foreign authorities
- The provision of extraterritorial jurisdiction needs to be used judiciously, as there can be situations where its use may turn a situation from bad to worse.
- Efforts should be made to promote international cooperation at different levels: bilateral, regional and multilateral.
- While there are enough justifications for a limited multilateral agreement on competition issues, the possibility of a non-controversial forum, other than the WTO, should be explored.

6

Interface Between Regulation and Competition Law

T.C.A. ANANT*
S. SUNDAR#

Introduction

The decade of the nineties has seen a paradigm shift in the approach to economic management in India. There has been a greater recognition of the value and significance in the use of markets and market friendly processes in the economy. The benefits of competitive markets are standard material for courses in economic theory. Equally it is well recognised that, for a variety of reasons, competitive markets may not exist or yield desirable results. The factors typically identified are externalities, economies of scale and scope, imperfect and asymmetric information, and imperfect competition.

Because of these different reasons for market failure, it is argued that crucial economic sectors cannot be left to unregulated markets and, a case is made for some form of intervention in the market process. The nature and character of the desired intervention would clearly depend on the source of the failure. But, for purposes of analysis we can classify two broad types of interventions. The first seeks to restore efficiency in a particular market through the creation of a sectoral regulator. Thus we have regulators in power, telecom, and the different elements of the financial sector, and so on.

The second seeks to create an entitlement for competition through a competition law, which seeks to promote competition and competitive practices in markets. The second type of intervention is

* Professor, Department of Economics, Delhi School of Economics, University of Delhi, Delhi

Distinguished Fellow, The Energy and Resources Institute (TERI), New Delhi

clearly most useful in correcting problems created by imperfect competition. The difference between the two forms of intervention is their nature. The first is clearly in the executive domain, with the regulator examining issues of technology, costs and processes in the regulated industry. The second is closer to an adjudicatory process, where the authority, either on its own or on receipt of complaints, acts on anticompetitive practices. It needs to be underlined that, as against the extant MRTP Act, the Competition Act, 2002 creates a proactive obligation on the Competition Commission of India, to promote competition in the market place. (see Chapter on Competition Act, 2002).

The separation between executive and adjudicatory functions are not perfect since competition authorities in exercise of merger jurisdiction, for instance, function in an executive capacity, and regulators are routinely empowered to adjudicate disputes amongst players on issues related to interconnect charges, access and so on. In addition to the functional separation, the sectoral regulator is typically narrowly focused whereas the competition agency has an economy wide remit. Here too, one must point out that some regulators, like environmental regulators, also have economy wide remits.

Instruments of Regulation

Typically regulators have a variety of powers to implement their brief. Thus, regulators can determine conditions of entry, as we see in professional services, such as Chartered Accountants, Lawyers, and Doctors. In each case the respective professional body regulates the qualification process through standards and certification (see Chapter on Professional Services).

The central/state regulatory commissions can issue licences for entities to be able to transmit/distribute/trade in electricity. In some cases however as in telecom, the power to regulate entry and/or modify licence conditions is with the government. The regulators, in addition, can influence conduct through standards and norms, as well as through explicit directions on prices, use of technology, and at times may even specify quantities that may be offered on the market. The exact choice of instruments is partly influenced by the characteristics of the industry, and partly by the objectives to be served. However different instruments require different types of information, and require different institutional structures at times to implement them. Different regulators have a different mix of powers allowed to them under the legislation. Thus in telecom, licensing conditions is a prerogative of the Government and, as we have noted in electricity, that power is given to the regulator.

Regulatory Failure

However sectoral regulators have been criticised on a number of grounds and these can be summarised as:

- **Narrow Technical Focus**: The technical and skill requirement of regulation imply that regulators are drawn from the industry they seek to regulate. This, at times, implies that they approach issues from their technical standpoint rather than the effect on social welfare. A related concern is one of regulatory capture.
- **Regulatory Capture:** The close proximity of the regulator to the industry being regulated, leads it to give higher value to the industries' requirements rather than those of consumers or market welfare. Furthermore, regulators who are dependent on the industry, to provide them with skills and personnel, are more vulnerable to capture.

  A consequence, of both these types of concerns, is that the regulator may not adequately take account of the requirements of efficiency and welfare. In addition to the limitations of a single regulator, the presence of multiple regulators, in closely related fields, leads to concerns arising out of regulatory overlaps.
- **Technological change/convergence/overlap**: Telecom, cable TV and internet service are increasingly seen as areas where the interests of different providers are in conflict. The potential conflict increases once we realise that optic fibre cables laid by the railways and electricity companies, also offer potential sources of competition. A similar convergence is seen in the financial sectors with converging interests of banks, insurance companies and stock market players. In spite of this convergence in the financial sector we see capital markets and insurance activities that were once regulated by

the Ministry of Finance, are now with Securities & Exchange Board of India (SEBI), and Insurance Regulatory and Development Authority (IRDA) respectively. Most Banks and Development Financial Institutions are regulated by the RBI. The Department of Company Affairs (DCA) regulates deposit-taking activities of corporate entities, other than banks and non-banking financial companies. Banking cooperatives are under the dual authority of the RBI and the various state registrars of cooperative societies. In telecom/media, the picture earlier was similar but, recently the government has nominated TRAI to be a unified regulator. Although separate regulators do exist under the Ministry of Information & Broadcasting for films.

The trouble is that different regulators have differing objectives, thus while the Reserve Bank of India is more concerned with systemic stability, the concerns of SEBI are investor protection and information disclosure. These may at times be in conflict. The other trouble with overlapping jurisdiction is that different regulators have different powers to enforce and punish.

A second problem is that the objectives of the regulator differ depending on the maturity of the market. Thus, the insurance regulator has a stated objective to develop the insurance market. Similarly the TRAI is obliged to increase tele-density. The market development objective, at times, requires the regulator to allow the regulated firms to make larger profits on existing operations, to enable them to meet the costs of market development. Thus, the approaches of a regulator, facing a mature market, may well differ from that of one facing an undeveloped market.

Regulation is often perceived to be gratis, available at no cost, but it is not so. There are costs of administering regulation; of compliance; and there are also structural costs. Excessive or inappropriate regulation can stifle efficiency. This leads to the natural questions as to what is the appropriate domain for regulatory intervention and to what extent can we leave matters to the free play of market forces.

Sectoral Regulators and the Competition Authority

The creation of a statutory competition authority raises additional concerns about the relationship between statutory regulators and the competition authority. In India, the relationship is somewhat ambiguous.

On the one hand, we have a very clear statement in the TRAI Act that it will be subject to the rulings of the MRTP Commission, and its power to determine entry, mergers or other matters relating to competition, are primarily recommendatory. The TRAI is directed to determine standards, and the terms and conditions, of inter-connectivity; technical compatibility and effective inter-connection; revenue sharing; quality of service; and compliance with universal service obligations. These have major implications for competition in the sector.

The Electricity Act creates ambiguities as the preamble clearly talks about the objective of promoting competition in the electricity market. The commission (central or state) is empowered to regulate production, supply or consumption, to promote competition and is further allowed to regulate distribution to prevent abuse of dominance. Thus, in its regulatory functions, the law clearly directs the regulator to act in a manner so as to promote competition and efficiency. Furthermore, they are also required to advise the government on measures to promote competition. In a similar manner, we see that in the financial sector, the RBI is authorised on all matters relating to bank licensing, mergers and practices.

On the other hand, the nature of the competition authority's power, vis-à-vis statutory regulators, is ambiguous. The law implicitly recognises that sectoral regulators have a role to play in competition matters, and says that statutory regulators may refer competition matters to the competition authority, but to what extent the competition authority can influence the regulators, in the absence of such requests, is not clear. This ambiguity runs the risk of creating either gaps or conflicts in the functioning of the respective agencies.

The practice in other countries has been to recognise these problems, and derive a variety of solutions for them.

In the UK, the Director General of Fair Trading, and each regulator are represented on the Concurrency Working Party, chaired by a representative of the Office of Fair Trading. The Working Party was formed, in 1997, to ensure full co-ordination between regulators and the Director General of Fair Trading, to consider the practical working arrangements between them. This includes ensuring that:

- a single case would not be investigated by more than one authority,
- to ensure consistency of approach in casework,
- to co-ordinate the use of the concurrent powers, and to prepare the guidelines.

In Australia, many of the utility sectors are regulated by the competition authority, and not by an independent regulator. On the other hand, there are competition agencies and regulatory authorities in some provinces, which are all members of the Utility Regulators Forum, where provincial regulators and competition authorities meet regularly to ensure better coordination. A similar forum exists in many other countries, including South Africa. In some other countries (Korea, for instance), statutory authorities are required to consult the regulator if they are planning any rule that may have an anti-competitive effect. Alternatively, the Competition Authority may represent its views before regulators (as in Canada, Denmark).

As we can see, a variety of different arrangements is possible. The key issue is to select one pattern and stay with it. The problem is that, in the absence of clear statutory or administrative rules/principles, it would be difficult to ensure compliance.

A logical question to ask would be whether we should exclude the competition authority from oversight, in all statutorily regulated sectors. This would not be desirable for three reasons:

- first, the possibility of capture alluded to above,
- secondly, the conflict between alternative objectives of the sectoral regulator, and the technical background of most sectoral regulators may make them poorly equipped to make assessments on competitive impact, and
- finally, the possibility of overlap across different sectoral regulators means that an economy-wide authority may, in fact, be in a better position to assess efficiency problems.

At the same time, it would not be prudent to exclude the sector regulators from addressing competition issues, in their sectors, as they would have a much better understanding of the sector than an economy-wide competition authority. The answer, therefore, is to provide for and encourage, cooperation between the sectoral regulators and the competition authority.

The problem arises because there is no uniform framework followed when we are designing regulatory authorities. Uniform guidelines are not adhered to, and it would be ideal if such provisions could be included in any law. It might be best to amend the Competition Act, to provide for cooperation between the competition authority and the sector regulators, and ultimately for the competition authority to have oversight in the regulated sectors on competition issues. Even in the absence of legal provisions relating to coordination, it can be achieved in a number of different ways:

- First, authorities can enter into formal cooperation protocols for sharing information and seeking advice.
- Secondly, to discourage forum shopping, we could consider a single appellate authority.

It should be noted, that in all these regulatory structures, the appellate authority will typically deal only with points of law rather than fact. Since the technical expertise is in the domain of fact assessment, there will be no loss of functionality by merging the appellate powers. In the UK, the Competition Commission hears appeals against all sectoral regulators' orders, thus promoting harmony and an economy-wide specialisation.

To sum up, we see that if the competition authority is to be successful, it must face up to the challenge of interfacing with sectoral regulators. Till this can be done statutorily, it should be pointed out that it could, and may be should, use its *suo motu* and advocacy powers, and represent, before sectoral regulators, on matters relating to competition concerns. Since typically all regulatory proposals are put up for public discussion, it would be useful for the competition authority to provide its input on them. For instance, the CERC has just issued a consultation paper on competition, and the competition authority should be providing official feedback using its powers of promoting competition and advocacy. The TRAI regularly publishes discussion papers on various issues, and many of them relate to competition concerns, and the CCI can send in its inputs.

RECOMMENDATIONS

- The Competition Commission of India should proactively participate in discussions on competition-related issues, before sectoral regulators
- Government should establish a concurrency party between the CCI and sectoral regulators, so that there is better coordination among them, to ensure that competition concerns are addressed properly
- In future, amend the Competition Act, 2002, with an enabling provision for cooperation between the Commission and sectoral regulators, so that it is not subject to arbitrariness

Part II

Competition Policy and Other Government Policies

7

Central Government Policies: Interface with Competition Policy Objectives

T.C.A. ANANT*
JAIVIR SINGH#

Understanding Competition

Competition, as widely understood in terms of the 'perfect competition' model with many buyers and sellers, and freedom of entry and exit, is not very helpful in serving as an overall guide to competition policy. The model is not universally germane to thinking about a competition policy, because the standard against which actual achievement would have to be measured and mimicked is hypothetical – a state which can only be achieved by altering the facts of the real world, in accordance with the ideal conditions and assumptions of the perfect competition model. Therefore, it is important to view competition more generally for our purpose, and one way of doing this is to discuss competition, not with reference to an outcome but rather as a *process*.

The *process* dimension of competition becomes obviously manifest, once it is realised that much of the ongoing economic activity is characterised by situations where it is not known beforehand as to who will do the best, and by using what means. Thus, competition is the *process* whereby skills and knowledge are acquired and put to the best possible use. In a liberal economy, if one were to look for such a policy emanating explicitly from *a* particular government agency or department, one would look in vain – typically, there is little likelihood of a 'Ministry' of Competition, though, of course, decisions made in each extant ministry would have an impact on competition.

* Professor, Department of Economics, Delhi School of Economics, University of Delhi, Delhi

Assistant Professor, Centre for the Study of Law and Governance, Jawaharlal Nehru University, New Delhi

The advancement of competition would be best found in the rights that form the basis of a liberal market economy. For instance, to provide an illustrative example, in the Indian Constitution the 'right to competition' can be inferred from Article 19(1)(g), which guarantees the fundamental right "to practice any profession, or to carry on any occupation, trade or business".

Approached from the perspective of rights, the notion of competition can also be thought of as incorporating, within itself, a sense of fairness – fairness in a procedural sense. This is clearly demonstrated by the fact that the presence of free competition is associated with the demand for a level playing field for all protagonists. Under free competition, a protagonist may win on account of some naturally possessed advantage of skills or technology, but not on grounds of privilege imparted to an individual or a group.

Understanding Government Policy

Even though the processes associated with competition can be legitimised by the guarantee of certain rights, such rights are typically not absolute or unfettered. Thus, subsequent clauses of Article 19 hasten to establish that the State can impose a series of 'reasonable' restrictions on fundamental rights in the interests of the public. Furthermore, the *Directive Principles of State Policy*, in Part IV of the Constitution, clearly set out critical elements of public interest. These include equitable distribution, equal opportunity, universal access to public goods, and protection of the environment. The point is that government policy is obliged to address issues, not only in relation to the processes in the economy, but also pertaining to the outcomes.

It is reasonable to say that, by and large, most government policies are oriented to effecting outcomes, rather than processes. The primacy of government policy, being oriented to generating outcomes, rests on the fact that these can be tangibly demonstrated and are amenable to being measured – poverty can be shown to have declined, tax collections to have gone up, erstwhile poor regions can be shown to have become prosperous, etc. Processes, on the other hand, are notoriously hard to measure and monitor. Assessing competition is much more a qualitative exercise than is the case with more outcome-oriented objectives associated with policy.

Central Government Policies: An Overview

The economic policies followed, after independence, had their roots in the prevailing ideology of the Indian National Congress (INC), during the Independence movement. While there were many strands to it, one clear element was to view markets as a colonial construct. The overall consequence of this *Weltanschauung* was a derogation of markets and market forces – a profound distrust of the use of market mechanisms to attain goals of the new state. Accordingly, a network of policies and laws, in a wide range of economic spheres, ranging from labour to foreign trade was put into place, which provided for a large and explicit role for the state.

Starting in the early 1990s, a combination of external and internal deficits forced the overall approach to the economy to be revised towards greater market orientation. As a result, it has come to pass that the industrial licensing system has been removed and bureaucratic control of economic activity substantially reduced. Policy documents put out by the Government, often enough, speak about the redefined role of the Government – for example, a 1993 document says:

"At the Central Government level, priority should be accorded to eliminating remaining barriers to industrial production, investment and import of technology, as quickly as possible. The Government's role should shift increasingly to restructuring unviable enterprises, ensuring fair business practices, safeguarding consumer interests, and minimising the adverse effect of industrialisation on the environment."[1]

In spite of this, a large overhang and backlog from the past persists in both attitudes and laws, which prevent the Government from construing and constructing policies, which are structured to work in sympathy with market processes. In some cases, this is not just a matter of the persistent past. Rather, the problem originates from a new source, but is approached with a conditioned and fragmented mindset, which is not appreciative of the nature of market processes.

To illustrate, consider some examples.

Trade Policy

- The older regime was marked with quantitative restrictions, tariffs, and an extremely intrusive and restrictive foreign

1. "Economic Reforms: Two Years After and the Task Ahead", 1993, Government of India, Ministry of Finance, Department of Economic Affairs 33

exchange regime. The last decade has seen significant relaxations in quantitative restrictions, reduction in tariffs and an easing of the exchange control regime. But, the operation of key elements of the trade policy regime have severe anti-competitive dimensions, for example, policies in relation to the operation of anti-dumping measures, intellectual property, etc.

Industrial Policy

- The pre-1991 industrial policy regime used to have explicit entry restrictions through a licensing policy, which, to all intents and purposes, meant that the state was operating a set of entry barriers. These barriers have been given up, but yet other barriers remain, using a variety of means. These originate, in part from zoning restrictions and environmental laws and, in part from the operation of the small industry reservations. The implications are that existing large firms are insulated from requirements under grandfather clauses, which act to subsidise their activities, and small industry reservation also acts to subsidise inefficient firms.

Public Sector Policy

- The earlier regime had created large public sector monopolies, which are currently being privatised, disinvested or converted to independent corporations. The terms of these purchases, nevertheless, require that the firms will continue to employ the existing work force and, at times, perform other 'social' obligations. In return, private purchasers often expect the state to ensure that the monopoly status and/or returns of the concern purchased will be maintained. Thus, for instance, in telecom, the public sector is compensated through Access Deficit Charges; and in power, through regulatory indulgence in tariffs and protection from "cream skimming".

Tax Policy

- The State has been attempting to introduce transparency and uniformity in rates and structures of taxation, which aim to minimise the effect on specific individuals. On the other hand, industries or sectors have been lobbying for preferential treatment and the practice of giving in to such natural political compulsions, by writing specific exemptions and breaks, have vitiated positive developments and created a non-level playing field. There is little attempt at assessing the competitive impact of alternative formulations.

Labour Policy

- The impact of labour policy on competition is one of the most interesting, and little appreciated, dimensions of public policy. The existing regime seeks to protect employment in the organised sector through an extensive regime of regulation. Leaving aside the matter of the inability of firms to easily make adjustments to their surplus work force, another facet of this regime is the unwillingness to let units close on account of poor performance. This implies that in the event of failure, strenuous efforts are made to revive the enterprise through soft loans, discretionary mergers, etc. This implies that one of the principal pillars of competition – free exit – is vitiated. Efficient firms face the additional burden of coping with state supported competitors. Quick exit is essential for the freeing up of resources and voiding unviable contracts, and requiring them to continue, as it impacts on the cost and performance of existing firms. A second dimension of labour policy is that the inspection regime, with its known weaknesses and corruption, constitutes a significant barrier to entry.

The point is that, as policy outcomes are sought to be generated, it is a persistent practice in India to do so without taking into cognisance that policies need to be framed, and implemented, in harmony with the market process, and not in a manner so as to stall the process. To phrase this differently, is to say that the Directive Principles of State Policy need to be implemented using modes that acknowledge the institution of the market, and not by either ignoring its presence or being antithetical to it.

Implications for Policy Formulation

If competition is to be privileged, then promoted outcomes should be generated in a manner that minimises the trade-off between furthering competition, as a fair process, and the impulse to shape fair outcomes. The trade-off, between competition, as a process, and government policy, as an outcome, needs to be analysed by appreciating the link between the robust functioning of the market and government policies. It is essential to realise that both the design and operation of policy instruments have an impact on the competitive process, by creating barriers to the process. To minimise the conflict, it is important to ensure that policy instruments are so engineered that market processes are not thwarted. This would require two broad principles to be followed: transparency and parsimony.

Transparency. Any policy that is pursued with the intent to engineer certain outcomes, in conjunction with the strategy employed to achieve the outcome, will result in a certain configuration of costs and benefits. It is paramount that these costs and benefits are listed openly, so that it is clear as to what extent the suggested policy is, indeed in the public interest, and to what extent it has been constructed to support some interest group, under the guise of supporting public interest. Therefore, the first step to be cognisant of the costs and benefits of a policy is to take measurements that will clarify the process of policy formulation: Who will benefit? Who is going to bear the costs? Apart from shedding light on these kinds of questions, such transparency vitally incorporates the market process in the discourse of policy formulation, since the calculation itself requires one to be mindful of the presence of the market.

Parsimony: If indeed the impacts of policy can be measured, then the policy to be put into practice needs to be designed in a manner that thwarts the competitive process the least. This implies keeping the policy tightly focused, with few and clearly enunciated ends.

While such transparency and parsimony, in policy formulation and implementation, is desirable across the board, it is useful to comment on these issues in relation to the *Competition Act, 2002* as an illustration in point.

Under Section 54 of the Act (the *power to exempt)* and under Section 55 (the *power to issue directions)*, the Government has the ability and the right to intervene in the processes of the Competition Commission. These powers imply that the Government itself is a significant player in the process of competition assessment. It needs to be particularly emphasised, in this context, that the power must be used in a framework that does not vitiate the entire exercise – the determination of public interest or sovereign power of the Government must be based on a coherent, transparent and parsimonious analysis, rather than relying on *ex-cathedra* doctrines of state rights.

Interestingly, in South Africa, if the Government has a view on a particular matter before the competition authority, which involves another policy dimension, it has to appear like any interested party, and make its views known through affidavits and arguments.

Within the structure of the *Competition Act, 2002,* it can be particularly recommended that under the clauses of the Act, the opinion of the Commission should be sought and utilised in a manner so as to provide for an effective competition assessment, of any major public policy or reform. Thus, for instance, a prior competition assessment, before privatisation, would lead to a more effective policy. The counterpoint to this, of course, is the ability of the Commission to undertake such assessments and make recommendations consistent with market processes.

The Head of the Korean competition authority, serves in the rank of a cabinet minister and, participates in all cabinet meetings. In this way, the Korean Government ensures that competition concerns are taken on board in all decision making. The Russian Minister for Anti-monopoly too serves on the cabinet. In many other cases, the Government hardly interferes with the processes of the competition authority, hence ensuring its independent function and better economic outcomes.

RECOMMENDATIONS

- Assess all laws and government policies on the touchstone of competition
- All government policies should have an explicit statement about the likely impact of the policy on competition
- Governments, at the union and the state level, should frame and implement policies by acknowledging the market process
- Government should evolve a system of 'competition audit' which could be applied to all existing and future policies

8

State Government Policies and Competition

PRABHAT DAYAL
MANISH AGARWAL*

Introduction

There are regulatory failures of state governments, or the policy regime leads to anti-competitive practices/outcomes at sub-national level. Unfortunately, these issues are most often ignored, partly because of lack of awareness and partly due to vested interests.

This chapter does a survey of five such issues, *viz.*, procurement policy, bid rigging in construction contracts, excise policy, truck operations, and retail services. In order to get inputs for the paper, a questionnaire was circulated to various experts and practitioners in the country. Approximately 30 responses were received.

Indeed, many of our Government policies are framed and implemented to promote competition, such as regulatory policies in the utility sector, or using import policy measures to offer competition. One incongruent policy is that on small-scale reservations. Closely linked with it are the state government procurement policies, under which price and/or purchase preferences are given to small-scale, as well as other, local units in the state.

Overall, these practices affect the competitiveness of local units to a large extent, and tragically remain unaddressed in public discourse. This is coupled with a huge number of regulatory failures.

Similar to happenings at the central level, the construction sector is scandalously infested with collusive bidding at the state level too, without any regulation. The mafia appears to dominate in most such

---

* Fellow and Policy Analyst, respectively, with the CUTS Centre for Competition, Investment & Economic Regulation (C-CIER)

businesses in the states and indulge in all types of anti-competitive practices, in collusion with politicians. In the area of goods transport, there is a mafia-led cartel in various places.

Another area is the state excise policy (revenue generation in liquor and other intoxicants), which is purely under state jurisdiction, and generates the second biggest revenue in the states. Here too, in many states, cartels of liquor operators exist. As a result, bids are suppressed and, state governments lose revenue in the process.

Besides, there are anti-competitive practices in the retail sector as well. Service sectors like barber shops, pan-biri shops, auto-rickshaw/taxi operators, etc., form unions and dictate prices.

Government Procurement Policy

In the federal set up that we have chosen to adopt, all States vie for the largest slice in the industrial pie. There is competition between states to attract maximum investment. States strive to put up packages for industrial promotion, wherein incentives like sales tax holiday, electricity duty waivers, and in various other forms, are given. Similar packages are devised to protect local units from outside competition. One such incentive is the preference given by state governments to local units in their procurement policy.

Several states have some government order or regulation, which gives preferential treatment in purchase to units situated within the State (Table 8.1). Under the policy, purchase and/or price preference is given to local units. Most often, the policy is targeted to protect and support small-scale sector units, which are presumed to be less competitive vis-à-vis large/medium industries. Even if the products of other units are competitive, they are not purchased. This is evident in the case of Andhra Pradesh, Karnataka, Madhya Pradesh, Rajasthan and West Bengal. The Government of Gujarat gives price preference to cooperatives.

These policies are designed to favour one class of enterprises over others, and distort competition between units producing the same product. In the context of the overall development policy of the state, such policies may be desirable. However, concerns arise, when the policy creates conditions for formation of a cartel of local manufacturers, which is solely dependent on Government's patronage. In such cases, the state government ends up paying a higher price for a product, which is often of poor quality. Moreover, with a captive market, where there is no quality control and no threat of competition, the enterprises may become uncompetitive.

The example of the barbed-wire association, in Rajasthan is a case in point. As per an earlier Rajasthan Government policy, a certain quota of barbed wire was to be procured from local manufacturers. This is supposed to have led to formation of a 'cartel' under the name of Rajasthan Barbed-wire Manufacturers Association. This association hiked the prices, and with an implicit arrangement, allocated the total requirement of barbed wire amongst its members. Consequently, poor quality barbed wire was procured at a high price, with almost no quality checks at the Government end. Local manufacturers depended solely on Government's patronage rendering them uncompetitive. With the changed Government procurement policy, local units closed down, and the association broke up.

The point is that whenever such policies are framed, which are designed to protect a class of enterprises, they should be prepared by acknowledging the market process. This is reflected in the policy of the new Government at the centre. Accordingly, competition is considered key to survival of Small-scale industries (SSIs). It is realised that SSIs cannot survive on Government protection and they need to work with a competitive spirit to face the increasingly globalised world.

Table 8.1

Procurement Policy of Select State Governments

S.No.	*State*	*Policy*
1	Andhra Pradesh	• Reservation of 17 products for purchase, exclusively from the local SSI units, which are registered with Commissioner of Industries in the Rate Contract System
2	Gujarat	• Price preference of up to 15 per cent to cooperatives
3	Karnataka	• Small-scale industry located within the State given 15 per cent price preference over medium, or large-scale industry
4	Madhya Pradesh	• State Government has established Madhya Pradesh Laghu Udyog Nigam (MPLUN) to promote SSI units and to market the products manufactured by them. • All purchases of state government, state public sector undertakings and local bodies made from units registered with the MPLUN
5	Rajasthan	• 80 per cent of the stores' requirement by all government departments and public sector undertakings to be met from local units, where the rates are not found competitive, even after grant of price preference and unit, from outside the State, is adjudged to the lowest.

Contd. ...

Contd. ...

S.No.	*State*	*Policy*
		• 60 per cent of this 80 per cent reserved for local SSI units, and remaining 40 per cent requirement to be met from other local industrial units. • Local units given relaxation of 50 per cent in earnest money. • Units within the State have their bids calculated excluding the State sales tax while outside State units have the Central sales tax added to their bid.
6	West Bengal	• Small scale industries enjoy a price preference of 15 per cent *vis-à-vis* large and medium industries, within state as well as outside the state

Another instance of regulatory failure arises from the incapacity of the State government, which culminates in anti-competitive outcomes. This is highlighted in the case of Orissa. There is a millers' cartel in Orissa, which is an outcome of the faulty procurement policy of the State government. The State Government collects raw paddy from farmers and sells it to millers for further processing, who sell the processed products back to the State Government. The Government of Orissa does not have its own processing industries. The millers capitalise on this and sell the processed products to the state government at a high rate. Ultimately, the Government sells the purchased product to the people at a very high cost. The procurement policy has, in this way, become miller-friendly instead of being consumer friendly.

Bid Rigging in Construction/Works

An area of government procurement where there are cases of collusion, is construction contracts undertaken by the Government.

As per industry estimates[1], during the last 5 years, all state governments together have spent around Rs 1,500,000 crore on civil works. In addition to this, about 800 Members of Parliament (*Lok Sabha* and *Rajya Sabha* together) annually receive Rs 2 crore each, under the MP Local Area Development Fund, for spending on projects/facilities in their respective constituencies, thereby adding Rs 1,600 crore annually. Add to this kitty, an equal amount that each

1. *Indian Construction*, Journal of Builders' Association of India, November 2004

Member of Legislature Assemblies (MLA), Member of Legislature Councils (MLC) and Corporator receives from the respective state government or municipal corporation, and the figure is around Rs 4,000 crore annually. The Bulk of this amount is spent on civil works, such as bus stands, foot over-bridges, health centres, clinics, hospitals, welfare centres, etc. Considering that the above is only a part estimate, since other infrastructure construction projects have not been taken into account, the total amount spent is simply mind-boggling.

All these projects are generally taken up by government agencies through the medium of contractors. Except in very rare cases, these works are awarded through a system of competitive bidding, which may be international or domestic.

Theoretically, the system of competitive bidding is sound. Notice inviting tenders, for a particular work, are published in international/national/state level newspapers. Depending on the complexity and quantum of the project, bids may be received in single or double envelopes. Bids are opened in front of all bidders, and the lowest bidder is determined through a transparent system and is awarded the work.

Be that as it may, this seemingly faultless system may not yield desired results, because of cases where contractors collude and there is a Tender-mafia at work. As a result of these distortions, competition is subverted and the bidding system fails to produce efficient results, even in cases where rules and procedures are properly followed. Most importantly, corruption in engineering departments is so deep that such practices are entertained rather than frowned upon. The nexus between contractors and engineers is well established. Rare exceptions do exist, when engineers are not corrupt, but they can hardly fight against the system, which is deeply entrenched.

The extent of the malice can be gauged from the fact that even the Parliamentary Standing Committee on Railways (2004), while discussing the question of procurement of concrete sleepers, observed, "The procurement of concrete sleepers has become a very sensitive matter, because a lot of unscrupulous, existing manufacturers have formed a cartel to secure orders by unfair means or tampering with procedure, and simultaneously keeping the new competitors out of the race. The Committee is constrained to notice that there exists a regional imbalance in the setting up of concrete sleeper manufacturing units. They also express their unhappiness that new entrants are not encouraged, which ultimately strengthen the cartel of old/existing manufacturers". In procuring 160 lakh of broad gauge sleepers, the Railways awarded contracts to the existing 71 firms, and ignored the 24 new firms entirely.

As per the industry information, there is now a trend towards awarding works in much bigger packages, which effectively rules out most small contractors from bidding, thus restricting competition[2].

In many cases, large contractors subcontract the work to smaller contractors, mainly because in large projects, it makes sense to subdivide work into smaller lots to make the project management task easier. This subcontracting is taken into account when the large bidders bid, and the profit of both the subcontractor and their own, is factored in. This leads to an escalation in costs of bigger packages. It is estimated that there can be a 10-15 per cent reduction in cost, if smaller contractors are not excluded from the bidding process. In Chennai, a flyover scam had rocked the state assembly, where contractors pooled up to share the contract at a considerable cost to the taxpayer. But nothing much came of it.

Angered by the malicious process, the Rajasthan Public Works Department (PWD) Minister announced in the assembly on July 20, 2004, that he would break all cartels, so that smaller contractors can bid for contracts. Subsequently, nothing happened, and it is now business as usual.

Other factors that hamper competition is the pre-qualification criterion, where, for bigger packages, past experience in executing similar works is a must, leaving the contract open for only a few construction companies.

There are good practices as well, which can be adopted to ensure competition in the bidding process. For instance, by selling tender documents through multiple sources. This has been tried in certain

2. "Awarding contracts in bigger packages for contractors does not necessarily reduce the total cost", Vijaya Raghava Reddy, Chairman, Builder's Association of India, Karnataka Centre, Bangalore, September 1, 2000 (http://www.indiamarkets.com/imo/industry/construction/constructftof1.asp)

contracts and has proved successful. The procedure creates uncertainty among the cartel members, as they are not sure how many bids have been submitted, and by whom. This makes it difficult for the cartel to monitor the number of bids outside the pool, and forces the members to submit reasonable bids.

Modus Operandi in Bid Rigging

The entire process of formation of collusion, among contractors while bidding is popularly referred as 'Pooling'.

The process starts with the closing date for purchasing the bid documents. Normally, a meeting is organised of all those who have purchased the bid-documents, and a decision is taken as to whom the contract will be awarded. The popular criteria for this 'selection', among others, include: (i) highest offer made for the 'pool' amount (ii) informal understanding among contenders to maintain rotation and ensure 'equitable' sharing of opportunities.

As per information, the 'pool amount' that the 'winner' has to contribute varies between 2 to 4 per cent of the entire value of the contract. This money is equally distributed among the members of the collusion. That way this parallel system works in quite a 'competitive', and 'democratic', manner!

More often, the departments concerned club smaller assignments together to make it a big one, for unknown reasons, which substantially reduces the chances of competitive bidding.

It is alleged that quite often staff/officials from these construction departments work in tandem with such collusions, and receive benefits. Even those who have been part of such collusion admit that 'pooling' cannot successfully be executed, without active support from within the department.

As per the information, such collusion works out in about 30 per cent of cases. Hence, figuring out 30 per cent of the total value of contracts being awarded, in recent years, will offer an indicative estimate of the amount at stake.

(Based on information gathered from personal interviews with reliable sources)

The Government of Andhra Pradesh's e-procurement scheme is another initiative to tackle the menace of bid rigging, and bring transparency in the entire procedure. It has helped a great deal in eliminating such practices, which were quite rampant earlier. As a result, there has been an increase in the number of average bids received from 3.4 to 6.7, besides generating significant cost savings of about 23 per cent. Given the success of this tool, all government departments in the State are expected to switch to the 'e-procurement' mode from January 2005.

Excise Policy

As per Article 246(3), of the Constitution of India, the Legislature of a State has exclusive powers to make laws for any matter enumerated in list II in the 7th Schedule, including production, manufacture, possession, transport, and purchase and sale of intoxicating liquors within the state. Item 66 of this list empower the State Legislature to impose fees in respect of any of the matters enumerated in this list. The excise duty is leviable in respect of alcoholic beverages, for human consumption, manufactured in the state or produced elsewhere in India.

The key objectives of excise laws are[3]:

Regulation

Under the Directive Principles of State Policy, Article 47 lays down that the State shall regard raising the level of nutrition and the standard of its people, and the improvement of the public health, as among its primary duties and, in particular, the State shall endeavour to bring about prohibition of the consumption (except for medicinal purposes) of intoxicating drinks and drugs, which is injurious to health. In view of this, the States are pursuing the policy of temperance and States like Gujarat have declared complete prohibition, whilst some other States like Tamil Nadu and Andhra Pradesh, have banned country liquor.

To regulate the production, manufacture, distribution, purchase and sale of liquor, elaborate rules have been made by all the state governments. Besides, state governments have the sole monopoly on the marketing of liquor.

State governments have adopted various systems for the distribution and marketing of liquor. This can be classified as:

- Auction system, wherein group of shops in particular area or individual liquor shops are auctioned for specific period;

3. Galundia, K.S., Study on Imports of Foreign Liquor (Post WTO Scenario), 2000

- Licensing system, where liquor shops are allotted on fixed fees, renewable on yearly basis;
- Wholesale trade by the state itself, and retail trade by individuals (Tamil Nadu, Andhra Pradesh, Karnataka);
- Wholesale trade by private parties, and liquor vends managed by the state (Delhi and Pondicherry).

State Revenue

Excise revenue from liquor is the second biggest source of revenue, after sales tax, for the state governments. State governments are collecting around Rs. 20,000 crore by levying duties and fees on alcoholic beverages. Government's policy is largely revenue oriented; the aim is to maximise revenue with minimum effort. All procedures, rules, etc, are determined, considering this objective.

Alcoholic drinks being a state subject, excise policies/duties/ licensing systems etc, are in the domain of the state governments. State governments have a plethora of rules and regulations, and often at variance with those obtained in other states. This has resulted in a number of anomalies, and also stunted the growth of the domestic alcoholic beverages industry. Such rules/policies govern licensing and regulations of distilleries/breweries, bottling units, warehousing, wholesale and retail sale, import and export, transport, pricing, labelling and packaging, locational instructions, registration of brands, limit on possession, duties and fees, etc.

In states where liquor groups comprising large geographical areas are auctioned for specific period, a number of malpractices and monopolies build up during the course of time. In this system, competition is restricted to few parties who have sufficient money, and muscle power, to carry out the business. Over time, it encourages cartelisation, at the time of auction, resulting in a monopoly in liquor trade, unhealthy competition amongst groups, and concentration of business in the hands of few licensees. As a result of this cartelisation, bids are suppressed and state revenues decline, as is evident in the case of Rajasthan (Table 8.2). The absolute figures show a marginal variation, but when adjusted with inflation, it shows a decline.

In its Excise Policy for 2004-05, the Government of Madhya Pradesh has decided to give up the system of allotting liquor sale outlets to the

Table 8.2

Excise Policy of Select State Governments and Its Impact

S.No	*State*	*Excise Policy and Its Impact*	*Annual Revenue (Rs. Cr)*		
			2001	*2002*	*2003*
1	Andhra Pradesh	• Prohibition fully lifted in 1997. • Ban on *arrak* (country liquor), while promotion of Indian Made Foreign Liquor (IMFL). • Marketing done through shops allotted on fixed charges by draw of lots. • Sale of toddy permitted only through toddy co-operatives • The Government itself controls wholesale trade through AP Beverages Corporation (APBC). *Impact of the Policy:* • Increased competition at retail level, but restricted competition at the wholesale stage • Significant increase in revenue	1243	1652	3261
2	Rajasthan	• State has been divided into 25 liquor groups, which generally tally with district boundaries. • These groups are auctioned as a single unit. • Until March 2004, RTDC was selling beer through its own shops. This has been discontinued. *Impact of Policy:* • Small bidders not able to participate in the auctions due to the size of the bid • With restricted number of bidders, only 11-12 liquor operators in the entire state, who have formed a cartel • State Government forced to lower the 'reserve price' repeatedly because bids suppressed by the cartel • Revenue has stagnated • No competition in sale of beer after closure of RTDC run liquor shops	1118	1110	1142

highest bidders through auction, and has substituted a lucky draw instead. According to the state Minister for Excise, this change in policy was aimed at subverting the liquor mafia, which, through its money and muscle power, was building monopolies in the liquor business. Uttar Pradesh had also adopted a similar policy from 2003-04 and the state's excise revenue jumped by over 30 per cent, as a result.

Truck Operations

Often truck operators, at district level or around major production centres, form a cartel, which then leads to increase in freight charges. In most cases, trucks that come in with goods are not allowed to carry freight from the production centre. In most cases, these cartels have local, or even state level, political patronage. There are innumerable numbers of such examples and some of these were also referred to the Monopolies and Restrictive Trade Practices (MRTP) Commission.

Truck operators' cartels result in higher transport costs since trucks bringing in goods charge two way fare, as they return empty, while transportation costs on out-going goods are about 40 per cent more. For instance, in case of Baddi, Himachal Pradesh, the Baddi Nalagarh Truck Operator Cooperative Transport Society, has monopolised the movement of goods from the state. Controlled by the local MLA, the truck union charges 30 per cent higher on the Baddi-Delhi route and 15-20 per cent on the Baddi-Mumbai route. Trucks coming in with supplies, go back empty because they are not allowed to pick up freight, which only adds to the cost.

There is an excise waiver for companies, in this industrial estate and a large number of consumer goods, and pharmaceutical, companies are setting up manufacturing units in Baddi. By controlling the commercial traffic in Baddi, the transport union has reduced the cost advantage the units would otherwise enjoy. Often, large companies find that cost advantage due to excise waiver is higher than the component of higher transportation costs, and are willing to yield to the blackmail of the local transporters. Small companies, however, are facing problems.

As per the information collected, Godrej Industries tried to bypass the truck union in Baddi, but this did not last long. Godrej, which has a manufacturing unit in Baddi, established a depot in Chandigarh. They used the Baddi truck union's trucks to transport goods from Baddi to Chandigarh but used other operator's vehicles for rest of the transit. However, this arrangement lasted for only a few days as the Baddi truck union learnt about this bypass arrangement, and refused to provide trucks to Godrej Industries. Godrej had to give in to their demands.

In the case of Orissa, transport cartels are formed with official backing. For example, the Angul Truck-owners Association, a duly Government registered body operating at the National Aluminium Co. Ltd.'s factory, charges as much as 200 per cent more for transportation of ingots, under the obliging eyes of the authorities. A complaint was once lodged with the district authorities against the association, but to no avail. Such official cartels are known to exist in other parts of Orissa also, like in Sukinda Mines, Paradeep Port and Balasore.

In a case in Alwar, Rajasthan, in the 1980s, the MRTP Commission had taken action against the local truck union, but with no success. An MLA, who later became a minister in the state, headed the local union. On the cries of the local industry, the issue came up before the district administration. The administration held that the practice followed by the union was not correct, and it was stopped only after concerted efforts.

On the other hand, Makrana in Rajasthan, was an unfortunate case as there was no action taken by district administration, and the stubbornness of the truck operators' union killed the marble business in this one-time capital of marble trade. Makrana had become a 'mandi', as marble blocks were transported from all parts of Rajasthan and were processed at Makrana. Later, truck operators formed a union and began exploiting the traders. The Union was charging tariff almost 35-40 per cent higher than the prevailing market rates. This led to an increase in transportation costs of marble from Makrana, and the usual harassment of dealing with a monopolist union. The harassment grew to such proportions that several marble-sawing plants moved to Kishangarh on the Jaipur-Ajmer National Highway No. 8. Gradually, more and more marble business moved to Kishangarh. As opposed to the 100 trucks, which used to come to Makrana, now hardly 35-40 trucks come. Kishangarh has become a rival mandi. Makrana lost its advantage and the town is gradually losing its prosperity!

The upshot is that any aberration at a local level can be tackled at the level of district and local administration. It requires willingness on the part of the administration to resolve the problem, taking a balanced view, after hearing all the parties concerned.

Additionally, companies can follow practices which rule out the formation of cartels. For instance, the Birla Cement factory in Chittorgarh invites bids for transport of goods through the Internet. It provides details of the trucks required on a particular day or week, and the destinations where the cement has to go. This helps the factory to get competitive rates, and cartels are thus compromised.

Regulatory Failures at Local Level

Cartel type activities are common in barbershops, car rentals, auto rickshaw rentals, and so on.

In most towns, taxi and auto drivers demand lump sum payments, even when meters do exist. The charges vary depending on location and also sometimes with the category of consumers. The case of Delhi is interesting in this context. Till very recently, a similar situation prevailed in Delhi with respect to auto drivers, who charged lump sum amounts. But now auto drivers in Delhi use meters. The reason for this sudden change: State Government has given clear instructions to the traffic police to *challan* auto drivers, who are found not using meters and cancel their driving licences. The result of this strong stance taken by the state government is easily seen on Delhi roads.

The basic problem is poor enforcement, which in turn is due to lack of political will. Moreover, in many cases, non-compliance costs are lower than compliance costs, as penalties fixed are unrelated to the extent of violations. By taking care of these factors, situations can change in favour of consumers, as shown in the case of Delhi.

Service sectors like barber shops; *pan-bidi* shops, etc, form unions and dictate selling prices, which are often above the printed price also. For instance, in Mumbai, the Pan Merchants Association decides and circulates a price list, which mandates members to sell at prices that are higher than those printed. This is a violation of the Weights and Measures (Packaged Commodities) Rules, but one cannot expect the weights and measures inspector to go around prosecuting every pan shop. Such type of practices needs to be dealt with, systemically, by the state government, but no one bothers! These are local issues and only local solutions will be successful in these cases.

In fact, most often service providers at the local level resort to these practices because of the need to grease the pockets of enforcement agencies at the local level. For instance, India Gate at New Delhi, where people go out for a stroll etc, is full of ice cream vendors in the evening. All of them charge more than the price printed on the package. Their explanation is that they have to pay "*hafta*" to the policemen on duty in order to sell at India Gate, where the business is brisk. Selling at more, than what is marked on the package, violates the Weights and Measures (Packaged Commodities) Rules, but the Department of Legal Metrology does not haul the ice-cream sellers up, and they continue to overcharge consumers. One wonders, why not use the same police force to enforce rules that favour the consumers. Their power can be used in a positive way to protect consumers rather than harming them.

Conclusion

Anti-competitive practices are rampant at the local level, and there is a clear need for state-level competition agencies, backed by appropriate laws, to tackle them. In fact, by promoting competition and effective regulation, the state governments can protect consumer interest as well as increase their own revenues. In other federal countries, like the USA or Australia, many provinces have their own state competition laws and agencies.

Such practices need to be dealt with, systemically, by the state government, but no one bothers. The lack of healthy competition and fair-trading in the marketplace affects the economy and consumer interest adversely. Thus there is a need for a local level competition regime to enable orderly markets, and add to economic growth.

RECOMMENDATIONS

- Create State-level competition and regulatory laws to resolve local level market abuses and regulatory failures
- Create awareness among all stakeholders, including state government officials, about the negative impact of these practices on government revenues and consumer interest
- Encourage the use of e-Procurement in bidding process
- Use local administration for better enforcement of regulatory practices

Part III

Competition Policy and Consumers

9

Competition Policy and Consumer Welfare

PRADEEP S. MEHTA*
RAJEEV MATHUR#

Introduction

The economic reforms initiated, since the nineties, through liberalisation, privatisation and globalisation, have brought about momentous changes in the structure of markets, in addition to transforming the employment scenario, income generation and consumption patterns of different sections of people. This has also necessitated changes in the legal regime-in the form of the scrapping of obsolete laws and enactment of new laws, suited to the economic reforms agenda in the era of globalisation.

One such legislation, which has been proposed to be scrapped and replaced, is the Monopolies & Restrictive Trade Practices Act of 1969, with the Competition Act of 2002. The earlier competition law was plainly out of synch, and thus the new competition law was adopted.

The main objective, of competition policy and law, is to preserve and promote competition as a means to ensure efficient allocation of resources in an economy, resulting in:

- the best possible choice of quality,
- the lowest possible prices, and
- adequate supplies to consumers.

To put it differently, ensuring competition is just a means to achieve the above-stated objectives. Obviously, maximising consumer welfare becomes a predominant concern.

---

* Secretary General, CUTS International
# Director, CUTS International

Therefore the need, for the Government, is to design and implement a competition policy, with the understanding that consumers need the invisible hand of the state to protect and promote their interests. Generally, competition policy has two elements:

- a set of policies that enhances competition in local and national markets: a liberal trade policy, relaxed foreign investment and ownership requirements, deregulation and privatisation, etc., and
- legislation i.e, competition laws designed to prevent anti-competitive business practices, and unnecessary government intervention.

However, it should be borne in mind that competition policy is just one of the tools, in the larger context of other overarching public policies and approaches, that also need to be addressed for promoting consumer welfare. The Indian consumer movement got an impetus with the enactment of the Consumer Protection Act, 1986 (COPRA) as it contains provisions for consumer representation and simple, speedy, inexpensive and informal justice to consumers, by means of establishing a separate redressal mechanism. There are fora at the district level, state level, and the apex National Commission at New Delhi. Each have a monetary jurisdiction and entertain appeals from the lower fora.

Further, the Act also aims to promote and propagate consumer rights, through the instruments of consumer education and establishment of consumer councils, at the state and district level, besides the apex Central Consumer Protection Council at New Delhi.

The Monopolies and Restrictive Trade Practices Act, 1969, was amended in 1984 to bring in consumer protection provisions, which dealt with unfair trade practices, such as deception, misleading advertising and claims.

Thus, the Consumer Protection Act, 1986, and the Monopolies and Restrictive Trade Practices Act, 1969, have been playing complementary roles in promoting consumer welfare in India.

Competition and Consumer Welfare

Competition means rivalry in the marketplace, which is regulated by a set of policies and law to achieve goals, namely, economic efficiency, check on concentration of economic power and consumer welfare. All these goals have an interactive relationship and, when in harmony, deliver total welfare. Indeed, the consumers are supposedly the biggest beneficiaries of competition. On the other hand, the consumers are the main losers due to anti-competitive activities in a market. The consumers are worse off because of their incapacity to deal with such problems.

In this context, it is sometimes argued out that competition policy and law are tools for the rich, the urban and industries alone. However, at the macro level, the design and implementation of a competition policy promotes the enhancement and welfare of the poor. At the micro level, an effective competition regime or consumer law (covering competition distortions) can prevent consumer abuses, both at industry level as well as in a village or locality where one shopkeeper can cheat the whole community. An appropriate and dynamic competition policy, and law, is imperative to buttress economic development, curb corruption, reduce wastage and arbitrariness, improve competitiveness, and provide succour to the poor.

Therefore the need for the government is to design and implement a competition policy, with the understanding that consumers need the invisible hand of the state to protect and promote their welfare.

Before we embark on assessing the consumer welfare implications, it is important to understand the notion of consumer welfare. Unfortunately, there is no agreed definition of consumer welfare. However, one can have a fair understanding of the notions surrounding consumer welfare by looking at the United Nations Guidelines for Consumer Protection, adopted by the UN General Assembly in 1985 and amended in 1999. It represents an international regulatory framework, for governments to use, for the development and strengthening of consumer protection policy and legislation, aimed at promoting consumer welfare.

The UN Guidelines call upon governments to develop, strengthen and maintain a strong consumer policy, and provide for enhanced protection of consumers, by enunciating various steps and measures, around eight themes. These eight themes are:

1. Physical safety
2. Economic interests
3. Standards
4. Essential goods and services
5. Redress
6. Education and information
7. Specific areas concerning health
8. Sustainable consumption

The Guidelines have implicitly recognised eight consumer rights which were made explicit in the Charter of Consumers International as follows:

- Right to basic needs
- Right to safety
- Right to choice
- Right to redress
- Right to information
- Right to consumer education
- Right to representation
- Right to healthy environment

These eight consumer rights can be used as the touchstones for assessing the consumer welfare implications of competition policy and law, and to see how they help or hinder the promotion of these rights.

Right to Basic Needs

In India, this right is the most crucial, because of high levels of poverty and deprivation. Thus, getting maximum goods or services out of a Rupee is more important for those who have less money to spend than those who have enough of it. By ensuring lower prices, competition can make basic needs more accessible to the poor. Moreover, the poor, who are engaged in agriculture and such other trade, are often not able to get the right prices for their produce due to anti-competitive practices of the buyers. Hence, if implemented properly, the Competition Act will make a significant contribution in this regard.

In this context, it is worthwhile to quote the World Development Report, 2000-2001:

"Markets work for the poor because poor people rely on formal and informal markets to sell their labour and products, to finance investment, and to insure against risks. Well functioning markets are important in generating growth and expanding opportunities for the poor people".

'Well functioning' implies markets that work efficiently and without distortions i.e., competitive markets where everyone has the opportunity to participate. However, 'competition' is often less understood, and easily distorted by players in the market, even when there are large numbers of them. Therefore, that competition laws are enacted to curb distortions.

Sectoral regulatory policies, which are an integral part of competition policy, also play a major role in ensuring the right to basic needs, for example, by mandating universal service obligations on the service providers so, that even at a loss, they will have to supply services to the poor and disadvantaged consumers at a reasonable price.

Right to Safety

Though competition policy and law do not directly deal with safety issues, they can make significant contributions in promoting safer products and services in markets. In a competitive market, sellers try to attract more customers, not only through cheaper prices but also through better quality, including more safety features wherever relevant. In a cartelised industry, there would be less innovation and less initiatives in improving safety standards.

Right to Choice

This is probably the most relevant consumer right, on which competition policy and law have important bearing. In pure and simple terms, right to choice means that there should be a range of varieties/producers available to consumers in each product and service. From this perspective, the 1991 amendment to the MRTP Act, which removed the merger review provisions, was a setback in this regard. This meant that the number of players would reduce, although this does not necessarily mean higher prices or anti-competitive arrangements. Nonetheless, the Competition Act is a significant improvement as it has merger review provisions. However, concerns have been expressed that due to high thresholds and voluntary notification requirements, these provisions may not be as effective as they should be.

Right to choice, however, has some other dimensions as well. Any restrictive practice has a bearing on consumers' rights to choice. A collusive market sharing arrangement is a prime example of this, where consumers have no choice other than buying from a particular seller. By including explicit provisions, the new Competition Act is likely to tackle such issues in a more effective way than the MRTPA. Inclusion of leniency provisions is another feature that would help identify, or expose, such practices prevailing in the market.

Certain types of unfair trade practices (UTPs) can also have an important bearing on right to choice. Misleading advertisement seriously jeopardize consumers' rights to choice. According to the MRTPA, offers of gifts could also reduce consumers' rights to choice. Gift offering is not necessarily an *offence*. When the cost of the gift is included in the transaction cost, and is against public interest, it is an *offence*. Promotion of a product through contests was also considered to be against the consumers' rights to choice by the MRTPC.

The MRTPC had restrained "Business India" magazine from continuing their sales promotion scheme of contests. An Investigation by the MRTPC investigating team revealed that the participants were induced to buy the magazine, on considerations other than their choice of participating in the contest. This practice not only distorted competition among publishers of magazines, but also deprived the participants of the benefit of other quality magazines available in the market. UTPs have however been put outside the ambit of the new Act.

Another dimension of choice is that, for marginalised consumers, it is restricted due to low purchasing power. From this perspective, lower prices of goods and services imply greater choice for these consumers. As already mentioned above, sectoral regulatory policies, with universal service obligations, also promote consumers' choice.

Right to Redress

The competition authority, with adjudicative power, in any country is an important component of the grievances redressal system. However, MRTPC, due to its inefficiency could not play this role effectively. It is expected that CCI, under the new Act, would be able to do better in this regard. The Act also allows for class action and private action, so that ordinary consumers and consumer groups would be able to use the forum for redressal of relevant grievances.

Right to Information

This is an important component of the MRTP Act as it has provisions for UTPs, including measures against misleading advertisements, which promote right to information. However, the new Act would not deal with such issues.

Right to Consumer Education

This is an area that has been neglected in the MRTP Act. However, the new Act is a significant improvement in this regard. It is indeed fortunate that the new competition law provides for competition advocacy, as one of its core areas of functioning. Under this the CCI will also need to generate awareness, and training programmes for all stakeholders. Awareness on competition issues among the stakeholders, including consumers and consumer organisations, is quite low whilst prevalence of anti-competitive practices is quite ubiquitous. Without proper education, it cannot be effectively tackled.

Right to Representation

There is no formal mechanism to ensure consumer representation in the implementation of the Act, though consumer representation was involved with rather significant impact when drafting it. Considering that the CCI will advise the Central Government on policy issues when asked for, this is an important deficiency. The CCI has formed an informal advisory committee where consumer organisations, such as CUTS, are represented. Maybe this can be formalised.

Right to Healthy Environment

Healthy competition promotes innovation. When firms engage in innovations, it often leads to reduced resource consumption, as they have to produce at lower costs to be able to compete. Reduced resource consumption would lead to environmental gains.

Some General Considerations

An area where competition law could be beneficial to the consumers, specifically the poor, is mitigation of the adverse effect of a strong intellectual property rights regime. Two sectors, namely pharmaceuticals and agriculture, are important in this regard. Coordination between the IPR authorities, such as the patent office, and the competition authority is necessary to yield such benefits. By using the compulsory licensing provision, an exploitative situation in life-saving drugs can be curbed. Similarly, in the agriculture sector, government interventions through judicious use of competition law, including cooperation with the competition law authorities in other countries, can help check exploitation by large agribusinesses who control most of the patents in seeds and biotechnology products. A major spin-off of such a coordinated action can culminate in pro-consumer technology development and innovation.

Competition Law and Consumer Protection Law

The previous section has already provided a few instances of how the MRTP Act has dealt with anti-consumer practices that are normally managed under a Consumer Protection law. This is because MRTPA and COPRA have overlapping jurisdictions, especially in the area of unfair trade practices. There are also several instances where competition or regulatory issues have been dealt with by the forums established under the COPRA. Here are a few examples:

- two photo studios in a small village in north India were penalised and stopped from exploiting poor and illiterate consumers by cartelising and abusing their dominant position;
- a bus transport company in south India was stopped from charging a higher fare, than the government approved tariff rates, on a particular route;
- in a class action against a big bank, it was ordered that it cannot discriminate between rich and poor consumers in providing service, during a strike, and that it has to maintain a skeleton service, at least.

The situation will, however, the very change once the new Competition Act comes into operation as it does not have provisions for UTPs, except for situations where businesses are affected by such practices that cannot seek redressal under the COPRA. A major concern that has been expressed, in this context, is that this will deprive the competition authority the opportunity to have a good public buy-in, as UTPs are closer to peoples' daily lives. They make headlines also. Forums under COPRA may, however, continue dealing with competition and regulatory issues, as many of them have a strong consumer dimension.

Conclusion

The benefit to consumers, from competition, depends on the efficient functioning of markets, without distortions, i.e., competitive markets where everyone has the opportunity to participate. However, 'competition' is often easily distorted by players in the market, even when there are large numbers of them. It is, therefore, important that a competition law is effective to curb distortions at all levels. It is thus obvious that the Competition Act may not bring the desired outcomes if it is implemented only from Delhi, or with some regional offices in addition, as there are anti-competitive practices that are prevalent at the grassroots level.

Forums under the COPRA have been dealing with such cases. However, this is not being done in a systematic way and, very often, the judgements depend on the personal perceptions of the chairpersons or the members concerned. One case of restrictive trade practice in Vijaywada, relating to tied-sales of school uniforms to students of a school, was treated as an unfair trade practice by the District Forum and then dismissed. It only showed the need to build the capacity of district forum members and chairpersons, so as to enhance their appreciation of the law. Such arrangements may be formalised through joint exercises, by the Competition Commission of India and the consumer disputes redressal fora. State level competition and regulatory framework should also be considered, as local problems need local solutions. Both in Australia and the USA, many provinces have state level competition laws.

As with many other countries, business is better organised and resourced, whilst consumers are unorganised and resource-constrained. This might pose a challenge for effective implementation of the competition law that promotes consumer welfare. Thus, it is absolutely essential to create and sustain a consumer movement, which will be well-resourced and empowered to advocate consumer interest and competition culture, and spread the same through research, training, lobbying, information dissemination and networking.

In order to do all this, consumer advocacy needs to be funded. For this purpose, there are several good examples in India, such as the Consumer Welfare Fund, which has been created out of excess excise recoveries, refundable to manufacturers. Other institutions like this also exist, and more can be created through imaginative processes. Moreover, competition advocacy would be more effective if consumer groups are closely involved in the process.

RECOMMENDATIONS

- Progressive legislation to suit the changing situations, arising from liberalisation and globalisation, should be encouraged to check abuses and improve consumer welfare
- The Competition Commission of India should jointly work with forums, under COPRA, to effectively deal with anti-competitive practices at the local level.
- Adequate mechanism should be made for consumer representation, on competition related issues, in a structured way.
- To help consumers, either directly or through policy interventions, it is imperative to create and sustain a strong civil society movement
- To create consumer advocacy funds, out of unclaimed money lying with various entities, on the lines of the Consumer Welfare Fund to enable the civil society movement
- To create state level competition and regulatory agencies to deal with local problems effectively, thus providing the easy access of justice to people.

10

Competition Abuses at Consumer Level: Study of Select Sectors

NITYA NANDA*
BHARATH JAIRAJ#

Introduction

Tied-selling is an anti-competitive practice that normally occurs when there is monopolistic dominance, or general scarcity in the market for some goods or services. However, this can also occur even if the market players act in collusion and all the players force such tied-selling.

Competition abuse, despite legislation, is rampant at the micro-level due to a variety of reasons, including difficulty in enforceability (as each player has an extremely small share in the overall pie), the 'status' of some of the service providers, and perceived quality concerns.

The present study looks at the anti-competitive policy of tied-selling in the secondary educational sector and the retail health sector. Surveys were carried out in five major cities (Delhi, Kolkata, Chennai, Bangalore and Mumbai) and five smaller cities (Jaipur, Lucknow, Bhopal, Vijaywada and Sambalpur) to glean a picture of the situation.

A total number of 734 education service consumers, 164 education service providers, 769 health service consumers, and 172 health service providers, were selected in these cities and surveyed.

The Problem

This study makes an attempt to understand the nature, extent, and impact, of tied-selling in health care and education services.

* Policy Analyst, CUTS Centre for Competition, Investment and Economic Regulation (C-CIER)

Legal Coordinator, Citizen Consumer and Civic Action Group, Chennai

The schools very often force the students to buy books, stationery and uniforms from prescribed shops/sellers, whilst the providers of health care services force the patients to buy medicines from prescribed pharmacies or get diagnostic tests done from prescribed laboratories. The issue is, of course, not so simple. Consumers may feel that they are paying higher prices on tied goods and services, while the service providers have their own reasons, like maintaining uniformity or quality, especially in the health care sector where authenticity of medicines or reliability of diagnostic tests are a concern.

School Education: Tied-selling of Books, Uniforms and Stationery

The survey found that nearly a third of schools (31 per cent) recommend or instruct their students to buy their books, stationery and uniforms from a particular place.

About 38 per cent of the consumers, who responded, thought that school authorities resort to such practices due to profit motives, whilst approximately 36 per cent thought it was for maintaining uniformity. About 22 per cent even thought that the schools might be attempting to provide good quality services, or making the items easily available to their students.

Interestingly, more than half of the parents (53 per cent) thought that it was unjust and unethical, on the part of the school authorities, to require the students to buy their books, uniforms and stationery from any particular outlet. Only about 23 per cent of the respondents did not find any problem with such practices. The remaining 24 per cent could not give their opinion on this. The low level of legal awareness is evidenced by more than half (54 per cent) the respondents, professing their ignorance on the issue. Only about 12 per cent of the respondents believed that there are laws to prohibit such practices, while 34 per cent thought otherwise.

Health Services

Tied-selling of Medicines

Overall, tied selling of medicines was not found to be a major problem, as only about 15 per cent of the respondents claimed that they had been asked to buy medicine from a particular shop. In Vijaywada (52 per cent) and Jaipur (40 per cent) however, the trend seems to be different. On an average, those visiting private doctors, or private hospitals, reported a higher incidence of the tied-selling of medicine. Service providers, though, indicated that such practices might be equally prevalent in government run hospitals.

On a positive note, nearly half of the people, who were asked to buy medicines from a particular pharmacy, found prices to be reasonable. This was not the original reason, though, to buy medicines from there and people mostly bought from there only to follow their doctors' advice or to 'not annoy' him/her. Interestingly, only less than two per cent of the consumers went against the advice of their doctor, and bought medicines from some other pharmacy. However, it should be mentioned that more than half of these people thought that the issue of better or genuine medicines was at stake here, leaving only about 36 per cent who thought that doctors did so with a profit motive.

When healthcare service providers were asked about tied-selling of medicines, only 11 per cent admitted that they ever resorted to such practices. Among them, about 84 per cent argued that they do so to ensure genuine and reliable medicines for their patients. When they were asked about others resorting to such practices only 17 per cent responded in the affirmative. However, interestingly, 35 per cent of them thought that 'other' doctors resorted to tied-selling practices with a profit or commission consideration.

Tied Selling of Diagnostic Tests

In the sample of respondents, slightly more than half of the people were asked to undergo diagnostic tests. Among these people, about half were instructed by the doctors to undergo the test at a particular laboratory, through either verbal instruction (46 per cent) or written instructions (48 per cent), and the rest were advised through nursing, or other, staff. As in the case of medicines, people visiting private doctors or private clinics reported a higher incidence of tied-selling of diagnostic tests.

The reasons for accepting the practice of tied-selling in diagnostic tests are illustrated below:

Reasons for Accepting Tied-selling of Diagnostic Tests

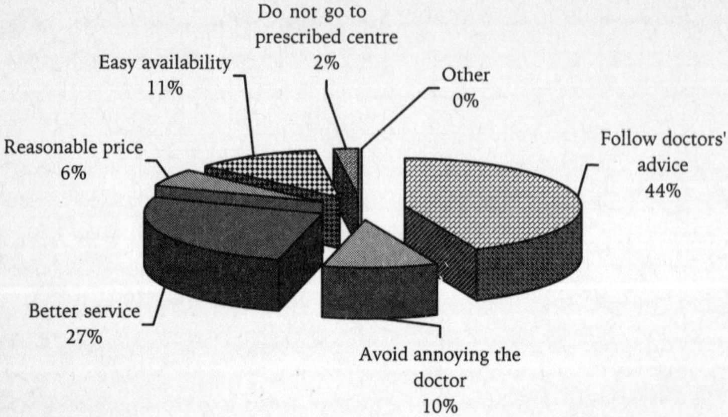

It is, however, interesting to note that though about 35 per cent of people thought that profit motive, on the part of the doctors, could be the reason for prescribing a particular test/diagnostic centre, an overwhelming 55 per cent thought doctors advised this to ensure reliable services. It is quite surprising to see that a greater percentage of consumers, as contrasted with the service providers, think that tied-selling of diagnostic testing is done to ensure reliability. Also, by and large, people seem to have confidence in the doctors, *vis-à-vis* the desirability or necessity of the test itself, as only about 16 per cent of respondents agreed with the view that doctors insist on too many tests.

Consumers with higher income have relatively less problems with such practices. This may be due to the fact that price differentials have less significance for richer people, and easy availability of the goods and services are more important to them. They might also feel that paying slightly more may be worthwhile, if the doctors have more confidence in a particular shop or a test laboratory.

When service providers were questioned regarding tied-selling of diagnostic tests, about 36 per cent admitted that they resorted to such practices, and 96 per cent of them argued that it was important to do so because of reliable testing services. More than half of them thought that other doctors/clinics do resort to such practices, but as many as 36 per cent of the respondents thought that their peers were motivated by profit or commission consideration. More than half, though, held that reliable service was also the main motive for other service providers. About 40 per cent of the respondents believed that such practices were justified and ethical, whilst an almost equal 42 per cent thought otherwise. Approximately half of them thought that these practices were not in conformity with the law of the land.

Interestingly, about 43 per cent of all the people interviewed regarded tied-selling practices, by doctors as unethical or unjustified. A high 30 per cent could not give their opinion on this, while about 21 per cent did not have any problem with such practices.

The Solution

Tied selling is a genuine concern that confronts several retail consumer sectors today. The information asymmetry between service providers and consumers, as indeed is the nature of their relationship, makes it impossible for the consumer to voice, let alone redress, a complaint. This is complicated by the fact that it will be difficult to expect the Delhi-based Competition Commission of India to monitor and regulate these practices, at the micro level.

One solution that can be put forth, with regard to schools, is that they might be able to offer value-added services by bringing together various products under the same roof. However, even in this case, schools should not be allowed to force students to purchase standardised products that are easily available in the market place. There could be a role for State Education authorities in drafting rules and guidelines on these issues.

A solution in the health sector is more complicated. For example, with regard to tied-in diagnostic services, more than half the patients believe that this is due to better reliability in testing centres recommended by the medical practitioner. Quality of medicines and reliable test results are extremely serious issues where problems can mean the difference between life and death. Regulatory frameworks exist to ensure quality medication, but enforcement is a problem. With regard to diagnostic testing, even the regulatory framework is absent. These aspects need to be kept in mind when trying to formulate any solutions to the problem.

The primary objective of this project was to look at anti-competitive practices at a consumer level. At this level, however, treatment tends to be symptomatic and not holistic. An in-depth study on other unfair trade practices and anti-competitive measures, adopted in the health and education sectors as well as in other retail sectors, is needed to understand the extent of the problem.

The capacity of consumer organisations to investigate and address such issues is also a drawback. Methods of strengthening this capacity, to investigate and document anti-competitive practices and to place such research before the Competition Commission of India or other relevant authorities, needs to be addressed.

However, there can no getting around addressing retail level anti-competitive practices, if we are indeed to move towards a healthy competition culture in the country. It is obvious that the Competition Commission of India has to be better equipped to reach out and provide more broad based, and holistic, answers to these problems.

RECOMMENDATIONS

- Carry out in-depth studies on other anti-competitive practices that are adopted in the retail/consumer sector, and expand on the study of the education and health sector.
- Strengthen the capacity of existing consumer protection organisations, and redressal mechanisms, to investigate and tackle retail anti-competitive measures.
- Competition Commission of India (CCI) to reach out to consumers, and sector regulators/authorities to create more awareness on competition issues at a retail/consumer level.
- State authorities to frame guidelines on selling of books, stationery, etc, by schools
- Establish a credible regulatory framework for diagnostic laboratories

Part IV

Competition Policy in Agriculture

11

Agriculture Markets in India: Implications for Competition

RAMESH CHAND*

Introduction

Markets for agricultural produce have expanded rapidly, after independence, due to the contribution of several factors, like increased production and increased commercialisation, development of communication and transport facilities, and the expansion of the market network.

As the distance between market places and production points decreased, the proportion of the surplus sold in markets followed a sharp increase. The share of commercial production in Indian agriculture has increased, and not even half of the production of major crops is retained for farm household consumption. This surplus part is disposed of through informal marketing channels, such as direct sales to consumers or sales in the village itself, and through formal channels of sales in nearby agricultural markets.

Role and Functioning of Agriculture Markets

The main role of agricultural markets is the delivery of farm produce from the source to the end consumer, and to provide price signals for resource allocation. The process involves several transactions, and logistics in terms of purchase, movement, processing, storage, distribution and transfer of property rights from farm gate to the consumers. If markets undertake these activities in an efficient and effective way, producers and consumers receive fair treatment i.e. producers obtain the worth of their produce and consumers get the value for their money.

---

* Principal Scientist, National Centre for Agriculture Economics and Policy Research, New Delhi

However, farmers generally believe that they do not get their due share for their produce, and that intermediaries corner the share of the consumer's rupee. At the other end, consumers believe that they pay much more than what an efficient and competitive market would require. To understand this anomalous situation, one needs to look at various activities/functions involved, in the transfer of produce from farm gate to consumers.

Typically, there are four stages in marketing agricultural produce, from producers to consumers, with agro-commercial firms operating as intermediaries. In the first stage, farmers, who have no influence on aggregate market supply, interact with agro-commercial firms; in the second and third stages, agro-commercial firms deal with each other; and in the fourth stage of marketing, agro-commercial firms deal with consumers, who exercise no control in the market.

Price Formation in Primary Markets

Prices for farm goods, for producers, are determined in the primary market, where the goods shift hands from farmers to an agro-commercial entity, such as trader, wholesaler, miller etc. These markets satisfy some important conditions of the competitive market, particularly on the sellers' side. This is generally not true on the buyers' side. This can happen if a single buyer or a group of buyers exercise market power, or, if there is some sort of collusion among the buyers.

In order to give fair treatment to farmers, the government took steps to bring all agricultural markets under the purview of Agricultural Produce Market Regulation Act (APMRA). Still, despite this institutional intervention by the government, which considerably diluted mercantile power in agricultural markets, there is evidence that primary markets are still not perfectly competitive. For instance, in a regulated market in Panipat, in the agriculturally advanced state of Haryana, evidence of collusion, in the purchase of *basmati* paddy/rice from producers, was found. Other evidence in various markets, in Coimbatore district, shows that entry barriers range from being low (millets) to considerable (cotton), and price information was secret, imperfectly available or open. There is also evidence of the common occurrence of excessive charges, deducted from producers, and the undercover methods of sale in some markets.

The state has responded to this situation by putting in place market regulations, and by providing alternative marketing avenues through cooperative marketing agencies and government agencies. The advantage accruing to farmers from the sale of produce, through cooperative marketing channels, can be seen from the illustration shown in Box 1. Besides providing better prices to producers, the main role of public/cooperative agencies is to improve the competitive environment in the market, by providing institutional alternatives to the market power of private traders.

BOX 1

Price Received By Farmers For Cotton in Warangal Market, Andhra Pradesh, from Sale to Various Agencies:

Sale Agency	*Price: Rupee/quintal*
1. Sale to Commission Agent:	710
2. Sale to Village Merchant:	700
3. Sale to Trader:	705
4. Sale to Cotton Corporation of India:	792
5. Sale to Miller:	785

Price Received by Farmers as Opposed to Price Paid by Consumer

The involvement of agro-commercial firms as intermediaries, in the transfer of agriculture produce from the farmers' end to consumers' end, leads to a difference between prices paid by consumers, or retail price, and prices received by producers, or farm price. This price difference, also called price spread, consists of the cost of (i) material and services, and net margins of various market functionaries, involved in the transfer of produce from producers to the ultimate consumers, and (ii) taxes and statutory charges.

There may be cases when the price spread is large and farmers' share in the consumer's rupee low, yet there is an improvement in the price realised by farmers.

Consider the example given in Box 2. When farmers sell mangoes, in the nearby local market, directly to consumers, they get almost 100 per cent of the price paid by consumers, as there is hardly any price spread. When the same produce is sold in the market through the wholesaler, who transports it to Mumbai, the growers get a mere 40 per cent of the price paid by the consumers. But this channel gives the growers a 13 per cent higher price than from the direct sale to consumers. Longer marketing channels, which sell produce where it gets a higher price, bring better return to farmers, even with a large price spread and a lower share in the consumer's rupee. The third channel represents the evidence in which the price spread is lower than the second channel, but both producers and consumers are better off than in the second channel. The reason for this, is that mango is marketed by a cooperative agency, which retains a very small margin.

BOX 2

Price Spread, and Farm and Retail Prices of Alphonso Mango in Different Market Channels in Maharashtra

Particular	*Producer-Consumer (Local Market):I*	*Producer-Wholesaler-Retailer-Consumer Mumbai: II*	*Producer-Cooperative - Consumer Mumbai: III*
1. Net price received by growers Rs/crate	161.27	182.00	264.00
2. Producer share in consumer rupee (%)	99.25	40.00	74.37
3. Net margin of wholesaler/ Comm. Agent		92.43	
4. Net margin of retailer		104.79	
5. Net margin of cooperative			37.77
6. Total marketing cost	0.73	75.78	53.23
7. Price spread	0.73	273.00	91.00
8. Price paid by consumer	162.00	455.00	355.00

Price spread depends on competition in the market, on its regulation and its implementation, and on technical efficiency of market functions like packing, grading, transportation, storage, etc. The greater the competition in the market, the lower the net margins and mark ups of market functionaries would be, and the lower the cost of market services and functions.

Several commodities produced in India lose their competitive edge to other countries due to the high cost of marketing, processing and transport. There are frequent violations of market regulation in order to charge excessive rates for various market functions. In some cases, in the grain market, labour unions dictate the produce handling charges and do not permit competitive rates. There are strong unions of truckers and tempo operators, in almost all towns and markets, who decide the freight rate, and other terms and conditions, with no respect for competition. Then, there are several regulations governing the movement of various goods, and multiple checkpoints, which are used less to ensure compliance but more for causing harassment and rent seeking. The net result is that the movement of goods, by surface transport, turns out to be very costly.

Further, statutory charges in the market, like purchase tax, commission of commission agent, *mandi* tax, etc, are the major sources of price spread. There is a lot of concern about the desirability and rates of some statutory charges. It is a growing feeling that service provided, in agricultural markets, does not match the heavy marketing charges, and these charges need to be curtailed to reduce the price spread and, ultimately, the burden on the consumer.

Retail Prices

At the retail level, business firms transact with non-commercial entities i.e. consumers. There are instances of market imperfections, collusion among sellers, and exploitation of consumers at the retail level. For example, in the case of cereals, pulses and edible oils, retailers do not display quality information about the produce. Consumers are fleeced through various kinds of adulteration. In the case of fruits and vegetables, neither the shops nor the hawkers typically display the price list. These retailers charge arbitrary prices from each consumer, based on his/her willingness to pay, and in the process, extract as much surplus as they can, rather than charging competitive prices.

In view of their market power, middle-men employ pricing strategies, which result in the complete and rapid transmission of an increase in farm prices to the retail level, but the slower and less complete transmission of a decrease in farm prices. This results in a strong asymmetry between wholesale and retail prices, which increase with the number of intermediaries.

In order to improve competition at the retail level, and to benefit consumers and producers, some innovative marketing mechanisms have been developed in some states. These involve direct sale of farm produce to consumers. They include *Apni Mandi* in Punjab and Haryana,

Rythu Bazaar in Andhra Pradesh, and *Uzavaar Sandies* in Tamil Nadu. Under these arrangements, farmers are allowed to sell their produce directly to consumers in the towns, on selected days and time, without intermediaries. Anyhow, the scale of operation of these marketing arrangements is quite small, as only farmers located in the vicinity of big towns can take an interest in this form of marketing.

State Intervention in Agricultural Markets

Functioning of agricultural markets shows that markets for large number of commodities are competitive, in the segment where agro-commercial firms are involved in transactions with other agro-commercial firms. Markets are less competitive where business firms are dealing with consumers and producers. The state has been intervening in agricultural markets, in various ways, to improve the efficiency of markets, and to ensure remunerative prices to farmers on the one hand, and reasonable prices to consumers on the other.

Statutory Regulations and Legal Provisions

In order to put a check on exploitation of farmers in the market, by various market functionaries, and to get fair treatment for them, the government took steps to bring all agricultural markets under the purview of Agricultural Produce Market Regulation Act (APMRA). These markets are called regulated markets and their principal objective is to safeguard the interest of producers, and to raise the standard of local markets where the exchange of agricultural goods takes place.

This law removed several unfair practices that worked against farmers and introduced standard codes weights and measures; rationalised market charges and specified methods for sale; transaction; and market conduct to impart competition, efficiency and transparency into the market. Furthermore, the law renders illegal any sale and purchase of agricultural produce outside the regulated (specified) market, or market yard, except where exemptions are granted specifically.

Experience in some states, especially in agriculturally less developed regions, shows that mere regulation does not help to improve market performance if adequate infrastructure is non-existent. It is reported that one third of the regulated markets in the country do not have common auction platforms. Infrastructure for marketing of perishables like fruits and vegetables, which require special facilities, like storage and processing, is hopelessly inadequate.

The strongest criticism of the APMRA is that it grants marketing monopoly to the state and prevents private investments in agricultural market. Secondly, it restricts the farmer from entering into direct contract with any processor/manufacture/bulk processor, as the produce is required to be canalised through regulated markets. Some provisions of this law, like purchase rights confined to licensed traders, have created entry barriers and thus reduced competition.

Because of these reasons the Inter Ministerial Task Force on Agricultural Marketing Reforms (2002) recommended that the Act be amended to allow for direct marketing, and for establishment of agricultural markets, in the private and cooperative sectors. The rationale behind direct marketing is that farmers should be able to sell their produce directly to agribusiness firms, like processors or bulk buyers, at lower transaction costs and in the quality/form as required by the buyers. In response to this, the Ministry of Agriculture, in 2003, prepared a new Model Act for agricultural produce marketing, which can be used by state governments to prepare their individual laws. Under the model act, the private sector can be licensed to set up market places. The model act also allows for contract farming and direct marketing by private trade.

The main aims of various regulations were:

- To check on the exploitation of producers and consumers by private trade through collusion, hoarding etc,
- ensure price stabilisation,
- raise the standard of markets and
- improve market performance.

Many changes have taken place in the marketing and trade environment since these regulations were framed. Development of transport and communication networks, expansion of marketing and increased competition in economic activities, have facilitated the increased role of the private sector in agricultural marketing. A feeling has emerged that numerous regulations have led to excessive control and intervention by the government, which are hampering the participation of private enterprises in agricultural marketing, and are proving counter-productive.

In order to increase the participation of the private sector in agricultural marketing, some changes have been made in the Essential Commodities Act (ECA) to remove the requirement of the licensing of dealers, and restrictions on storage and movement of food grains, sugar, oilseeds and edible oils. Similarly, the Sugar Control Order, and the Milk and Milk Product Order have also been amended to allow more freedom, and increased participation by the private sector in marketing of these commodities.

Price Administration

Principal components of price administration are:

- price support and procurement,
- maintenance of buffer stock and operational stock,
- public distribution system, and
- open market operations.

These interventions have served the purpose of food security, maintaining price stability, and the creation of favourable pricing environments. Of late, these interventions have come under severe criticism. Minimum support prices (MSPs) are found to have served only particular regions, and most of the crops and states could not benefit from them. Government procurement has created a perverse environment for the private sector, to avoid buying from farmers and to prefer buying from government, which is burdened with excessive stock and food subsidies. The government's procurement, distribution, and buffer stock programmes are reported to have had a negative impact, of repressing private foodgrain marketing, undercutting its potential contribution to long term food security. This is further said to discourage modernisation of marketing, resulting in losses and inefficiencies. Uncertainty about government intervention in grain markets, in terms of procurement and open market sales, in some cases, results in hoarding by private trade.

The Way Forward

The functioning of agricultural markets shows that markets for large number of commodities are competitive, in the segment where agro-commercial firms are involved in transactions with other agro-commercial firms. Markets are less competitive where business firms are dealing with consumers and producers. This is reflected in collusive behaviour of the buyers, and imperfections at retail level. This calls for improving competition in agricultural markets, particularly at the farm and retail level. Alternative avenues for sale and purchase, through cooperative marketing agencies, are found to dilute market power of private trade to some extent. Besides cooperative agencies, removing all kind of restrictions on entry of private firms, at various levels of agricultural marketing, particularly in purchase of farm produce, would help improve competition.

Legal provisions, like ECA, restrict the participation of the private sector. These laws were relevant to check hoarding and other exploitative practices when there were scarcities and markets were segmented. With the improved availability of various commodities, and the development of communication and transport networks, markets are getting spatially and temporally integrated. This environment is conducive for expanding business enterprises and promoting competition. This can be achieved by removing various obstacles in conducting business in agricultural produce.

Under the present Agricultural Produce Market Act in India, state governments alone are empowered to initiate the process of regulating agricultural markets. This prohibits the private sector from taking any initiative in to set up a modern market infrastructure that requires high investments, entrepreneurial skills, and managerial capacities. The provisions of the Act need modification to facilitate the private sector, and the cooperatives to establish agricultural markets.

Contract farming is being promoted in several parts of the country to raise the income of farmers through production of high value crops, better marketing opportunities, and scale advantages. In several cases, the contracting firm wants to directly procure produce from the farmers. Yet, in most of the states and in most agricultural commodities, these direct sales are illegal as the produce is required to be sold only in the notified market area. In such cases, changes in legislation are needed to take full benefit of contract farming. This would reduce market costs and increase returns to farmers.

In some states, taxes and charges on agricultural produce are quite high. There are reports that, to avoid these market charges, produce is diverted without entering into the regulated markets. These charges need to be rationalised and should commensurate with the services rendered in the market.

There is considerable scope to reduce the price spread, by improving transport and processing facilities. Similarly, increased participation of the private sector in agricultural marketing is needed to promote competition. This requires removal of restrictions, like licensing, etc; and the introduction of a favourable, regulatory and legal environment for private enterprises in agriculture. Government interventions in influencing market prices, that distort demand and supply or create uncertainties, vastly dampen private sector participation in the market, which ultimately hurts consumers.

There is no effective regulation at the retail level of agricultural commodities. Quality and price aspects are hardly displayed. Retailers charge prices, based on customer's willingness to pay, and in the process, extract as much consumer surplus as they can, rather than charging uniform and competitive prices. There is a need to frame and implement regulations, providing complete information about product quality and prices, to consumers through visual display. In order to provide more competition at the retail level and to benefit consumers and producers, innovative marketing mechanisms like *apni mandi* and producer's sales counters, in consumer centres, should be promoted.

RECOMMENDATIONS

- Innovative marketing mechanisms can be employed for direct sale of farm produce to consumers, *viz,* Apni Mandi, and producers' sales counters in consumer centres
- Make necessary changes in the legislative provisions to facilitate the private sector, and cooperatives to establish agricultural markets
- Contract farming should be promoted to reduce market costs and increase returns to farmers
- State taxes and charges in agriculture produce need to be rationalised and should commensurate with the services rendered in the market.
- Improve transport and processing facilities; and promote investment, in infrastructure through private participation, to reduce price spread.

Part V

Competition Policy in Manufacturing Sector

12

State of Competition in the Indian Manufacturing Industry

K.V. RAMASWAMY*

Introduction

The concept of competition can be defined in many ways. Here competition refers to rivalry between firms, in a market, for objects like market share and profits[1]. Market power is the ability to raise market prices, above competitive levels and exclude competition.

We need to distinguish between competition in, and competition for, a market. Competition *in a market* refers to actions of incumbents in an established market, and those potential entrants who would like to sell the same product. The instruments of competition would be price or capacity (quantity competition) and other non-price instruments, like new products, advertising etc. This involves erecting entry barriers, product differentiation, research and development, vertical integration, etc.

Competition *for a market* is defined as a process of creating a new market, based on innovative technologies and/or new standards (example: new operating system for Windows). This involves challenging the sellers of existing products, through the introduction of new products or creating potential competition, by upfront investment in facilities, to supply a new product. Here, the instrument of competition is not the price or capacity.

Measurement of competition *for a market* is much more difficult than the measurement of competition *in a market*. Here, our focus is

* Associate Professor, Indira Gandhi Institute of Development Research (IGIDR), Mumbai

1. This is a working definition which we shall use without getting into technicalities and rigours of economic theory.

on assessment of the extent of competition, in markets, in the Indian manufacturing sector. We examine the existing recent evidence, on the state of market structure, market conduct and market performance, to understand the extent of competition in Indian Manufacturing.

Manufacturing Sector in India: Size and Structure

The manufacturing sector in India is still relatively small. The share of the manufacturing sector in GDP has remained more or less stagnant in the 1990s (Table 12.1).

Table 12.1

*Share of Manufacturing in GDP**

Industry	*1993-94*	*1996-97*	*1997-98*	*1998-99*	*1999-00*	*2000-01*	*2001-02*
Manufacturing	16.1	18.2	17.7	17	16.7	17.2	16.8
Registered	10.5	12.3	11.6	11.1	10.8	11.2	11.1
Unregistered	5.6	6.0	6.1	6.0	5.9	6.0	5.8

Note: * 1993-94 prices

Source: National Accounts Statistics, 2003

Trade and Industrial Policy Liberalisation in the 1990s

The industrial and trade policy reforms initiated in the 1990's have substantially altered the state of competition in Indian manufacturing industries. Some of the changes made:

Removal of Legal Barriers to Entry

The foremost instrument of industrial policy was the industrial licensing for private entrepreneurs, based on the Industries (Development & Regulation) Act of 1956. The new industrial policy of 1991 abolished industrial licensing, except in 18 industries. In 1993, the passenger car industry was delicensed, followed by white goods, and the entertainment electronics industry, in 1996. The sugar industry was delicensed in 1999. At present, only six industries require compulsory licensing. They are potable alcohol, tobacco products, electronic aerospace, defence equipment, and drugs and pharmaceuticals.

Removal of Capacity Expansion, Takeovers, and Merger Restrictions on Large Firms

The barriers to entry for larger firms, put in place by the Monopolies and Restrictive Trade Practices Act (MRTP) of 1969, and the Foreign Exchange Regulation Act (FERA) of 1973, have been removed.

Raising Foreign Equity Participation

Equity participation greater than 51 per cent, is permitted on a case-by-case basis and the nature of production activity. This was later liberalised, to enable setting up of 100 per cent subsidiaries in the manufacturing sector, without any restriction on the number of such subsidiaries.

Removal of Protection to Small-scale Industries (SSIs)

A number of products, which were under the Small Scale Industries reservation policy, have been removed from the list. Most recently, 75 items were dereserved in 2002-03. Yet a large number of products (more than 700) are currently reserved for exclusive manufacture by SSI enterprises. The budget 2004-05 has sought to remove another 85 items from the reserved list.

Easing Access to Foreign Technology

Technology imports are permitted, subject to the following conditions:

- lump sum payments should be below Rs 10 mn,
- royalty below 5 per cent on domestic sales and below 8 per cent on exports,
- the total outgo from the date of agreement, is below 8 per cent of sales.

Restrictive clauses, such as foreign exchange cost balancing, applicable to consumer goods such as (a company's foreign exchange earnings must cover the cost of purchase of technology), have been removed.

Trends in Market Concentration Over Time

What has happened to concentration levels in different industries, in the post-reform period, in the Indian manufacturing sector? Have the concentration levels declined, compared to the pre-reform period?

We have examined the changes, in concentration, for selected industries in recent years. The selected industries may be grouped under the following three broad categories: (1) consumer non-durable goods (2) consumer durable goods and (3) intermediate goods. The measure of concentration is the Herfindhal-Hirshchman Index (HHI). The estimates of HHI are taken from the CMIE database called Market Size and Market Shares[2].

Consumer Non-durable Goods

The Consumer non-durable goods sector comprises of food, beverages; soaps; textile products, like apparel and footwear; and certain electrical products, like lamps & tubes. Market concentration has increased in three key consumer goods industries namely: biscuits, synthetic detergents, and lamps & tubes (See Table 12.2).

Table 12.2

Consumer Non-durable Goods Industry: Changes in HH Index of Concentration in Selected Industries

	Industry	*1993-94*	*2000-01*
1.	Biscuits	0.05	0.14
2.	Soaps	0.05	0.05
3.	Synthetic detergents	0.15	0.19
4.	Lamps & tubes	0.14*	0.16
5.	Infant foods	0.30	0.38
6.	Malted milk foods	0.40	0.46

Note: *1995-96

Source: Market Size and Shares, August 1999 and August 2002, CMIE

Consumer Durable Goods

Oligopoly is the market structure of many consumer durables' industries. The Concentration level has increased in four industries, namely, automobile tyres, mopeds, motorcycles and bicycles. All the

2. CMIE estimates the HH Index by taking the shares of all companies in the domestic market. It is not adjusted for the market share of imports. Reliable market share data has always been and continues to be scarce. Market share is more subject to errors in industries where a large unorganised sector co-exists with the organised segments. This is prevalent in industries like biscuits, lamps & tubes, air-conditioners, steel furniture, air-coolers and domestic electrical appliances.

four industries have one major firm with a high market share. MRF (market share 24 per cent) in automobile tyres; Hero Honda (market share 50 per cent) in motorcycles; TVS Motors (market share 46 per cent) in mopeds; and Hero Cycles (market share 40 per cent) in bicycles.

Intermediate Goods

Under intermediate goods, five of the ten industries show a decline in the concentration levels. One industry, namely, television picture tubes, showed no change. Two industries, belonging to the industrial category textile fibre intermediates, namely, polyester staple fibre (PSF) and viscose staple fibre (VSF), have a substantial increase in the concentration levels. In paints & varnishes, three firms jointly have more than 63 per cent of the total market. These are Asian Paints, Goodlass Nerolac and Berger Paints.

The markets for manufacture in India were subject to tariff and quota protection for many years. In the 1990's, India liberalised its trade regime by reducing tariff barriers and removing quantitative restrictions on imports. Tariff liberalisation, in the 1990's in particular, has been dramatic. Imports, as percentage of GDP, have risen to above 15 per cent at the end of the 90's.

No study appears to have been undertaken to analyse the impact of foreign direct investment (FDI) and competition in Indian manufacturing. Available data, on industry-wise distribution of FDI, indicates a major share of FDI inflow has gone into engineering, electrical and electronics, and chemical industry groups. FDI and the entry of transnational corporations are reported to have increased competitive pressure in a number of industries, like beverages, food processing, passenger cars, consumer durables and electrical equipment. Careful studies of the impact of FDI, and Mergers and Acquisitions (M&A), on competition, are required to understand the state of competition in India in recent years.

Relative price movement, that is the average rate of increase in the price of an industry, relative to the rate of increase in the manufacturing sector, is a key index of the rigorous competition in individual industries. Some studies have estimated relative price

3. It also reflects the relative change in demand and supply conditions.

changes at an aggregate level, that is, at two-digit national industrial classification. This is shown in Table 12.3. Seven of the eighteen industries show a marginal increase in relative prices. The wood products industry records a substantial increase. The remaining ten industries record falling relative prices.

Table 12.3

Relative Price Movement in Indian Manufacturing – 1990s

	Industry	*Relative Price Change for 1991-1996*
1	Food products and beverages	0.85
2	Machinery & equipment	0.86
3	Electrical machinery	1.04
4	Paper & paper products	1.07

Conclusion

The changes in market structure, in manufacturing, show a mixed picture. In the key industries, 12 of 30 sectors showed an increase in concentration, whilst three did not show any change, and the rest of the industries showed a decline. Import penetration rates were found to be low and negligible across industries, except in the chemicals industry. It was noticed that the lowering of average tariff rates and the removal of non-tariff barriers across industries, had substantially reduced the levels of protection to Indian industries.

What also came to the forefront, was that both domestic and foreign-owned firms have taken dominant positions in many industries. Market concentration has risen, in several industries, as a consequence. The increase in advertisement to sales ratio, along with R&D to sales ratio, suggests that firms are increasingly resorting to strategic competition. Many dominant firms are facing both price and quality competition in their industries.

RECOMMENDATIONS

- Research on sources of persistence, of dominant firms in individual industries, and the stability of market shares
- Study links between the state of competition, in input markets, and the state of competition, in product markets.
- Conduct case studies, of industries with new entry, and the response of incumbent firms
- Analyse the impact of FDI on competition in the Indian industry
- Further study Inter-state trade and tax regulations, and their impact on competition of different industries
- Look at the impact of environmental regulations on the competitiveness of firms
- Carry out a series of studies defining markets and market boundaries
- Linkage between industry, trade and FDI date should be established and maintained on a continues basis

13

Competition Issues in the Indian Cement Industry

PRADEEP S. MEHTA*
NITYA NANDA#

Introduction

From 1914 till 1924, the cement industry in India was at a nascent stage and the sector had high import dependence of more than 50 per cent. The industry showed signs of growth during 1924-41, with severe competition amongst producers, depressing prices and profitability. It was at this juncture that several cement companies came together, to create a common identity, under the Associated Cement Company (ACC), to mark the first move towards consolidation.

Probably to undo this move, the British Government in India brought production and distribution of cement under its direct control in 1942, citing defence needs, in the wake of the Second World War. The control of prices, however, continued even after the war. The Essential Commodities Act, 1955, recognised cement as an essential commodity. Pursuant to this, the Cement Control Order was introduced in 1956 to control both price and distribution of cement.

Such a heavy control of the industry resulted in its sluggish growth. Realising this, the government announced partial decontrol in 1982. This resulted in an extensive modernisation and expansion drive. Encouraged by this, the government introduced total decontrol of cement in 1989. In the next two years, the industry enjoyed a boom in sales and profits. In 1991, the economy went for large-scale

* Secretary General, CUTS International

Policy Analyst, CUTS Centre for Competition, Investment & Economic Regulation (C-CIER)

reforms. Nevertheless, the next couple of years were not good for the industry. Of late, cement companies have been doing well. In the year 2003-04, production in the country surpassed 117mn tonnes with the capacity utilisation level reaching almost 85 per cent. This trend is expected to continue in the future as well, considering the Governments' commitment to boost infrastructure and economic reforms.

Table 13.1

Cement Industry – Key Figures (million tonnes)

	2002-03	*2003-04*	*2004-05 (P)*	*2005-06 (P)*
Capacity	132	137	141	148
Consumption	108	113	122	132
Exports	3	3	4	4
Production	111	117	126	137
Surplus/Deficit	0.3	0.9	0.7	0.7
Cap utilisation (%)	84.4	85.7	89.7	92.1
Consumption growth (%)	9.0	5.2	7.2	8.0

Nature of the Industry

India is the second biggest producer of cement in the world, only after China. There are 125 large plants owned by 54 companies. However, cement factories are clustered in a few locations, depending on the availability of raw materials, namely coal and limestone, as both are bulky items that make transportation difficult and uneconomical. Proximity to big markets also plays an important role in this regard as the final product is bulky as well. Most limestone deposits in India are located in the states of Andhra Pradesh, Chhattisgarh, Gujarat, Madhya Pradesh, Maharashtra and Rajasthan, leading to the concentration of cement units in these states.

Due to the very nature of cement (being very bulky), and incurring huge transportation costs, manufacturers tend to sell cement in the nearest market first, and in distant markets only if additional realisation is greater than freight costs incurred. This highlights the regional nature of the cement industry. The Indian cement industry is normally viewed in terms of five regions: north, south, east, west, and central.

The southern region is the largest market, both in terms of consumption and installed capacity. The southern market is also quite insulated from competition from other markets, due to geographical location and transport costs. The eastern market is also quite isolated. Most of the plants in this region are concentrated in the state of Jharkhand, which is located in the extreme west of the region, from where they serve markets in far off places, like the northeastern states. Thus, it is quite difficult for plants located in other regions to serve this region. The western region is the one most open to competition from other regions as some plants in the southern, northern and central regions can serve it. Other regions are served from their neighbouring areas to some extent.

Traditionally, the Indian cement industry has been characterised by a large number of small manufacturers. Though, the consolidation process over the last few years has led to the emergence of a few big players. The top six[1] players hold about 60 per cent of the total capacity, whereas some 46 odd competitors together hold the rest. The median installed capacity of these units is just 0.86 of the total capacity. Looked at from the regional perspective, the size distribution is even more skewed. For example, Lafarge, the sixth largest competitor in India, is the largest in the eastern market. The cement sector is relatively shielded from international markets. Being a very bulky item, international trade of cement is very limited, and only occurs between neighbouring countries.

Table 13.2

The Major Players

Producer	*Capacity in 2002-03 (million tonnes)*	*Share of Total Capacity (%)*
Grasim-L&T	29.9	21.51
GACL-ACC	28.2	20.32
India Cements	8.8	6.34
Madras Cements	5.0	3.58
Century Textiles	4.7	3.24
Lafarge	4.5	3.24
Top six players	81.1	58.37
Remaining capacity	57.8	41.63
Median capacity	1.2	0.86

1. Considering that the combinations of Grasim-L&T as well GACL-ACC are to be treated as one player, though legally each are different companies.

Competition Concerns

Consolidation is not an entirely new phenomenon to the Indian cement industry. However, in the financial year 2001-2002, consolidation in the sector gained pace. International players find India's expanding cement market a lucrative playing field, as the current demand in the Indian market is set to cross its installed capacity very soon. While a few multinationals have been eyeing the Indian market, Lafarge and Italcementi have already made their foray.

The takeover of L&T by Grasim, and the strategic alliance between GACL and ACC have resulted in two major blocks, controlling over 42 per cent of the domestic market share. Before this major consolidation, the top five cement majors in the domestic industry accounted for 30 per cent of total capacity. Post consolidation, the top five companies account for more than 55 per cent of the total cement capacity in the country.

Despite the significant consolidation in the cement industry over the last few years, the size distribution remains highly skewed. Obviously, a large number of companies are operating much below the efficiency scale. From the market competition point of view, it would have been far better if, for example, Grasim took over a dozen smaller companies rather than L&T's cement business.

There are views that, indeed, these cement giants should grow further as cement business is capital-intensive and therefore a business of scale. While the largest Indian player, Grasim-L&T has a capacity of about 30 MnT, the largest player globally is Lafarge with a capacity of 150 MnT. However, production capacity as well as the market of Lafarge is spread over different countries of the world. Grasim-L&T is an Indian company, with a very small share of its production going to export markets. Moreover, it is also questionable if such a structure gives Lafarge any cost, or efficiency, advantage or market advantage only.

It is well known that the likelihood of attempted collusion, as well as its success, increases as the number of players involved becomes smaller, and as each one's leverage in the market share increases. Both these conditions appear to prevail in the Indian cement industry today, and hence, the authorities need to be vigilant to prevent anti-competitive practices in the market.

It is widely believed that the cement manufacturers are engaged in collusive price fixing, since the beginning of the decontrol of cement prices, in 1989. Indeed, this could be a legacy of the erstwhile control regime, when the Government essentially determined the price. Nevertheless, after decontrol, the cement manufacturers came together under the Cement Manufacturers Association (CMA) to lobby for higher prices. As a consequence, discussing prices has always been an important part of their collective lobbying activities. It would not be surprising if they continued with this, even as the government withdrew from price determination.

The cement industry, after all, is known to be prone to cartelisation worldwide. Cement, being a low value bulky good, is more or less immune to export competition, in major relevant markets, as the transportation cost is very high. The product being nearly homogeneous, fixing the price does not pose any major problem. The possibility of cartelisation in India gets strengthened as the market is fragmented, and few sellers dominate each of the fragmented markets.

In 1991, the Indian cement industry was formally accused of price rigging for the first time. The MRTPC was asked to adjudicate on a matter of collusive price setting in the Delhi market. The decision, though, went in favour of the industry.

The allegation of collusive practices came forcefully again in 2000. Cement manufacturers stopped despatches all over India from November 27, 2000, to December 3, 2000. Despatches resumed from December 4, but with a uniform price hike all over the country. Leading cement manufacturers: GACL, ACC, L&T and Grasim were perceived to be acting as a cartel. The Builders' Association of India (BAI) reacted by demanding government intervention to initiate action under the MRTP Act for "unfair trade practices" resorted to by the cement industry. They approached the central government to reduce import duty as well as withdraw the additional special duty and countervailing duty.

The MRTPC initiated a *suo moto* enquiry into the cement price hike that took place between November 27, 2000 and December 3, 2000. Cement manufacturers, on the other hand, denied any cartel type arrangements. They claimed that the price hike was the result of an increase in the cost of manufacture of cement. Cost of raw materials and inputs went up due to royalty charges, including a hike in coal prices, thus making the cement price hike essential.

BAI, on their part resorted to the selective boycott of cement manufacturers. The Government also responded, to the demands of the BAI, by slashing the import duty in the 2001-02 budget. Subsequently, prices of cement started falling throughout the country. In fact, in the western market, prices fell even below the previous level. It is not known if good sense prevailed upon the cement majors; or Lafarge, who refused to play ball with the domestic players, especially in the eastern market where it is the biggest player, triggered such disunity; or, it was because of the actions of the BAI and the Government.

Allegations of price collusive behaviour, within the cement industry, continue to be raised time and again. There are, of course, good reasons for making such observations. As can be seen from Table 3 below, the southern region has a huge excess capacity, both in absolute as well as in relative terms, and yet the average price prevailing in the region is higher compared to other regions. It also had the highest increase in average price in the year 2003-04 compared to 2002-03. In the western region, the average price had a fall, even though it was quite low compared to other regions.

Meanwhile, the MRTPC lost its vigour due to the adoption of the new Competition Act. It is not known if any case was lodged with the MRTPC, or if there was any progress in the case initiated by the MRTPC, as noted above.

The recent events in the industry have shown that it is not difficult for new players to enter the market. Although, this can be done only through the acquisition route, in the short run. The gestation period of installing a cement plant is fairly high. Coupled with this, is the fact that, competition from import is extremely limited. On that account, the market is contestable in a limited sense.

The Indian cement market had a reasonably good number of players. Despite the recent trend towards consolidation, dominance by a single firm is not yet perceived to be an important issue. Hence, no case of predatory pricing, or such other anti-competitive behaviour arising out of dominance, has been reported so far.

Table 13.3

Region-wise Capacity and Price Movement

Region	*Installed Capacity (million tonnes)*	*Total cons. 2003-04*	*Excess Capacity*	*Relative Excess Capacity*	*Price (2002-03) per bag in Rs.*	*Price (2003-04) per bag in Rs.*	*Price 2002-03 and 2003-04*
Northern	25.20	22.60	2.60	11.50	136	142	4.0%
Eastern	21.71	16.95	4.76	28.08	141	146	3.4%
Southern	44.30	31.65	12.65	39.97	139	145	4.6%
Western	25.33	22.60	2.73	12.08	133	132	-0.9%
Central	20.99	16.95	4.04	23.83	127	128	3.4%
Total	**137.53**	**112.75**	**24.78**	—		—	—

One important aspect of the Indian cement market is that nearly 30 percent of the total cement consumption in the country is in the government sector. The governments (both Central and State) buy cement, in bulk, through competitive bidding. Anyhow, there are good reasons to believe that such bidding procedures may be subverted by bid rigging.

Conclusions

The increasingly concentrated industry, faces larger and larger risks of firms resorting to collusive practices and uncompetitive behaviour. In order to protect the economy and consumers from collusive behaviour, and other anti-competitive practices, the new competition law is required to be implemented vigorously.

The MRTP Act, 1969, did not have merger review provisions. The new Competition Act, 2002, has these provisions and such activities will be subject to surveillance. As has been noted before, there is sufficient scope for further consolidation in the industry as there are many small players. Consolidation among them should rather be encouraged to improve efficiency. Nonetheless, further consolidation among the bigger players should be carefully watched and may not be allowed.

On the issue of cartelisation, however, no credible action has been taken, despite repeated allegations to that effect. The weak provisions in the MRTPA, along with weak investigative capacity, due to resource constraints, among other extraneous factors, are the primary reasons for cartel formation going unchecked for years. The new law is a significant improvement in this regard, with clearer provisions and leniency programme.

Admittedly, proving collusive behaviour would be an uphill task for the new competition authority. There is, however, one important source of information that may be explored. Careful analysis of offers, by different companies in Central and state government bids, can give important clues if there have been patterns of systematic rotation of winning bids, stable shares of companies in overall procurement, etc. This information would also be helpful in detecting collusive behaviour in the market as well.

RECOMMENDATIONS

- Competition Commission of India should analyse the cases of cement and other cartels, which could not be disclosed under the MRTP Act.
- Comparative analysis of countries where cement cartels have been successfully discovered, with that of India
- Careful analysis of the bid offers, discovered by different companies in central and state government contracts, can give important clues if there is any collusive behaviour
- Rolling programme on the analysis of the cement price movements, in regional markets
- Encourage consolidation among small players to improve efficiency, but carefully analyse further consolidation among the bigger players

14

Competition Scenario in Indian Steel Industry

A.S. FIROZ*

Introduction

Steel is a heterogeneous industry, with widely differentiated products, varying technology and economics. The competition issues in this industry, in India, have specific characteristics, and not all of them can be accommodated in a general framework.

Competition issues are to be seen, in general, in the context of (a) the market or pricing power of a firm (or a segment of the industry), and (b) the size of the firm. The first issue relates to market competition, including market share of the firm, and its ability to control market price; and the second relates to mergers & acquisitions, the ability of firms to mobilise investments and other resources, etc. This second point is important in the context of entry barriers, and the industry's possible transformation into acquiring a monopolistic, or oligopolistic, character because of such initiatives.

A Historical Overview and Emerging Scenario

Steel was a controlled sector till 1992, and the erstwhile policy was to allocate scarce resources for optimum development of the industry, and to make this critical industrial intermediate available at reasonable prices. The sector's growth was also determined, within the overall policy framework of the government of having a strong public sector. Though the private sector was kept out of the major integrated blast furnace based plants, other steel making

* Chief Economist, Economic Research Unit, Ministry of Steel, Government of India (Views expressed are personal and are being expressed in this paper in pure academic pursuit).

technology routes, and downstream re-rolling, were allowed in the private sector, but within the licensing regime. The Government, through the Joint Plant Committee (JPC), controlled steel prices and regulated distribution of the main steel producers. Although such a system should have favoured consumers, in effect it did not with the trading intermediaries taking full advantage of the price gaps that existed between the administered and the market prices. A black market operated in the steel sector for a long time, which was encouraged by concerned vested interests.

The control regime in steel, as also in other sectors, was proving to be holding up the industrial and overall economic growth, especially in view of the shortage of investment funds, with the government to raise capacity in the controlled industries. The government has since 1991, progressively opened up the steel sector for investment, both to domestic and foreign private capital, and completely abolished the price and distribution control. With a host of other economic reforms in related areas, the steel industry found itself in a competitive environment for significant, growth-attracting, private investment. The public sector behemoth, Steel Authority of India Ltd (SAIL) was corporatised to provide a level playing field.

Competitive Structure of the Steel Industry

Steel is produced in India, using a variety of technologies in plants with extensive size and quality variation, and in various levels of process integration. Technology and command over raw materials, through direct ownership of iron and/or coal mines, put the major steel producing companies in different states of intra-industry competition. The policy related to the lease and operation of iron ore and coal mines, has been significantly liberalised allowing for substantial ownership by the steel plants.

Table 14.1 shows the comparative percentages of installed crude steel capacity in India, between 1997-98 and 2003-04 (total installed capacity 39.28 MT). The percentages can be taken to represent the actual comparative output and the market share, as the influence of the market share changed between 1997-98 and 2003-04. Whereas in keeping with financial constraints the share of SAIL dipped, and the share of small units increased substantially, reflecting the government's pro-active policy. Anyhow, since steel products vary by size, shape, physical & chemical properties, criticality of end application, etc, and plants have limitations, on account of diseconomies of scale and technical constraints, competition for each gets confined to only a small number of players. It makes little sense, therefore, to consider competition in the steel industry as a single distinct phenomenon.

Table 14.1

Crude Steel Capacity

(in Percentage)

Unit/Year	*1997-98*	*2003-04*
SAIL	37.81	30.68
TISCO	9.64	10.18
RINL	8.53	8.85
Essar	6.95	6.11
JVSL	4.96	4.00
Ispat	3.79	4.58
Lloyds	1.42	1.15
Other EAF/MBF	3.89	9.07
IF	23.00	25.38
Total	**100.00**	**100.00**

To understand the market/competition forces at play in the steel industry, however, it is not necessary to study each such interplay, and it is enough to examine one or two representative cases.

Among the flat products: the Hot Rolled Coil (HRC) is one of the most critical products of the industry, not only because of economies of scale (hence large investment) required for its efficient production but it is also the single largest steel product traded (Total production ~ 13 MT). Five producers: SAIL, TISCO, JVSL, Essar and Ispat, together, have a share of 93 per cent production and 90.6 per cent on domestic merchant basis.

SAIL and TISCO also manufacture downstream products, though these capacities are not able to consume their entire HRC production, and much of it is merchandised. They also add to their saleable product mix. JVSL and Ispat do sell HRCs to their downstream units/

sister concerns, but strictly on a commercial basis (i.e. within the definition of merchandising).

This scenario, though *prima facie* made to order for cartelisation, is restrained for the following reasons:

a) The threat of imports. This is already 6 per cent of the total consumption, and with import duties at a low level of 5 per cent, the pricing power of the domestic producers is considerably reduced.

b) The public perception about the importance of steel in the nation's life

c) Most of the users of HRCs are medium size firms, but together they constitute a fairly large lobby.

Points b & c above force the government to intervene, sometimes indirectly, to stabilise prices.

A further bone of contention in the above scenario is that the downstream producers have often to compete, with the major producers, for the same end-product market. But, there are complaints that the differential price between the intermediate and the end product, quoted by the latter (probably to protect its market), does not cover conversion costs and squeezes the former.

Another important intermediate is the billet/pencil ingot. The main producers are SAIL (including IISCO), TISCO and RINL. Together, they control about 21.1 per cent of the market, but it is doubtful whether they can influence the market with any significance

Last but not least, is the matter of government policies affecting the competition scenario. Till very recently (January 2004), the import duty was 25 per cent. Also till recently, the major steel producers benefited from floor prices. Some procedure related non-tariff barriers, like mandatory BIS certification of imported steel, and designating certain ports for entry of certain categories of steel, were in place, adding to transaction and transportation costs, including those arising out of cumbersome delays.

Cartelisation

Although there seems to be no strong evidence, or possibility, of cartelisation, suspicions of concerted action by the steel majors –

especially the privately owned units – continue. It is true that they have sometimes got together to decide on prices, but these are perhaps more as a response to external pricing alternatives, than to seek rents out of dominance. Here too, they sometimes end up competing with each other with differential rates of discounts, offered by individual sellers. The PSUs are at some disadvantage, having to remain range bound under political compulsions. Their mandate to publish monthly price lists may be used as benchmark prices by the other players. With a conscious policy decision to remain outside of any sort of cartel, and with a market share of only 30 per cent, their pricing decisions are unlikely to affect the market significantly, and they may finally end up being merely market followers. At the end of the day, it can be said that there is a modicum of cartelisation when the market is strong, but not when it is weak.

Finally, since prices are based on the best alternative cost principle and there is a limit to an efficient mill continuously increasing capacity to grab market share, there is no incentive to reduce price to seize a larger share of the market. Furthermore, since the inefficient firms do not die (soft budget constraints), such moves will be matched with impunity. Therefore, it is prudent for the mills to work out common pricing at all times.

Competition Issues in the Context of Investment and Growth

Capacity creation in the steel industry involves large investments towards plant, machinery and infrastructure. Obviously, any infrastructure development under government auspices, especially selective area-based infrastructure development, has a large bearing on the investment environment, and the competitive position within the industry. Further growth of steel firms will also largely depend on their control over raw materials - mainly iron ore and coal mines. The government policy, in this regard, will have significant implications on this. For example, the policy followed by certain state governments to allocate iron ore mines, on a captive basis, to firms setting up plants (only in that state) will adversely affect the competitive growth of individual firms, and at the same time lead to inefficient allocation of resources.

Two major avenues of funds generation in the steel industry are through the capital market, and bank finance. If such funds create excess capacity, that is again well spread out, the steel market will turn hugely competitive for the benefit of consumers. If not, a monopoly or oligopoly will result. Table 14.2 below gives the actual and projected crude steel capacities between 2003-04 and 2011-12. It is seen that in 2011-12 the percentage share of each player evens out a little.

Table 14.2

Projected Crude Steel Capacity

Unit/year	*2003-04*	*2011-12*
TISCO (Jam'pur +)	4.1 (10.25)	10.5 (16.6)
SAIL (+IISCO)	12.1 (30.25)	15 (23.7)
RINL	3.5 (8.75)	6.8 (10.8)
Essar	2.4 (6)	4 (6.3)
JVSL	1.6 (4)	4 (6.3)
Ispat	2.4 (6)	3.6 (5.7)
Mini Mills	14 (35)	19.3 (30.5)
Small EAF/Small BOF	4 (10)	6.7 (10.6)
Small IF	10 (25)	12.6 (19.9)
Total	40 (100)	63.2 (100)

The role of banks and other financial institutions is important, in this context, as the primary source of funds. In the absence of any standard efficiency criteria for the steel industry, banks, nevertheless, tend to fund reliable, financially strong and established units only, in order to ensure the safety of their own funds, possibly ignoring the merits of smaller and fresh entrepreneurs, thereby indirectly nurturing monopolistic tendencies.

Regulatory Authority

The government announced, recently, that a regulatory authority could be set up for the steel industry. The steel industry has a long history of price and distribution control. At the current conditions of the market, and given the commodity nature of steel, it is neither possible, desirable, nor practical to have a regulatory body of the kind seen in areas like energy and telecom. It may, however, be useful to have a monitoring body involved, essentially with competition and allied issues within the industry, especially on the supply side of the market, particularly, in the areas of investments, mergers and acquisitions, ownership of mines, etc.

Conclusions

The steel industry is a highly heterogeneous and fragmented industry, with differentiated size of individual units, products, etc.

Whereas integrated steel plants are capital intensive, and dependent on basic raw materials and infrastructure, the smaller mills are dependent on scrap and intermediates from the integrated plants. Intra-industry competition is complex due to merchant operations, where the consumers of intermediates face competition, with the same finished product also produced by the producers of the intermediates.

The economics of scale of the industry do not permit the efficient production of basic steel from plants, below a critical size. Imports are the most important source of competition, but in the past, this has been maintained in favour of domestic players by direct state intervention and high levels of protection. The levels of protection have, on the other hand, declined in recent times. Financial institutions have to be more objective in the matter of sanctioning loans.

The idea of a regulatory authority does not make any sense, as the world over, competition in the goods sector is overseen by the competition authority of the country concerned. What the government needs to do is enable competition to prevail in the market, by using trade policy, tax policy and industrial policy, to ensure that there is adequate supply, and producers do not indulge in restrictive trade practices.

RECOMMENDATIONS

- Fiscal and trade policy measures for the steel should continue to keep a check on domestic prices.
- Mandatory publication of steel prices by the PSUs extend undue advantage to private firms and should be dispensed with.
- A fair and equitable policy, towards allotment of iron ore mining leases, for captive consumption is needed.
- Mining leases should be conditional, on minimum phased utilisation of the capacity, so that supply of the mineral is not affected due to deliberate idling of mines.
- Banks should follow a merit-based project funding policy rather than get totally guided by prospects of recovery, assessed *ex ante*, to avoid excessive concentration of public investment funds in a few companies.
- Instead of a regulatory body on steel prices, the Government should launch a rolling programme for continuously studying the competition issues in the sector

15

Competition Policy for the Pharmaceuticals Sector in India

NITYA NANDA*
AMIR ULLAH KHAN#

Introduction

The Indian pharmaceutical sector has come a long way, from being a small player in 1970, to becoming a prominent provider of healthcare products, meeting almost 95 per cent of the country's pharmaceutical needs today. As per an estimate by McKinsey & Co, the pharmaceutical industry in India has a unique and exciting opportunity to grow from about US$5.5 bn in 2000 to US$25 bn in 2020.

However, there are doubts in some quarters if further growth and internationalisation of the industry, in the changed scenario of a new patent regime and a deregulated environment, will benefit the common people by providing better access to affordable medicines. Since 1970, the prices of essential drugs have been regulated by the Drug Prices Control Order (DPCO), with the National Pharmaceutical Pricing Authority (NPPA) fixing the prices of a range of drugs, since its establishment in 1997. Even though, over the last few years, a substantial decontrol of prices has taken place.

Nature of the Pharmaceutical Industry

The usage of pharmaceuticals in India is governed by four primary medical sciences: Allopathy (modern science), *Ayurveda* (an ancient Indian Science, mainly using herbal remedies), *Unani* (practised largely

* Policy Analyst, CUTS Centre for Competition, Investment & Economic Regulation (C-CIER)

Fellow, India Development Foundation, Gurgaon

by the Muslim community), and Homeopathy, with allopathy being the most popular. This paper focuses on allopathic medicines only. The pharmaceuticals market is broadly divided into bulk drugs (20 per cent) and formulations (80 per cent). The pharmaceutical sector is a high-technology and knowledge-intensive industry. The industry has a two-tier structure. The largest firms account for the majority of the R&D investment in the industry, and hold the majority of the patents. A large number of smaller firms manufacture off-patent products, or those under licence to a patent-holder.

The organised sector accounts for 70 per cent of the industry in terms of value. The top ten companies account for 30 per cent of total sales. The individual market shares of companies are small. Though, this does not mean that there is intense competition in the market. This is because pharmaceutical products are not single, homogeneous goods, and there are a huge number of "relevant markets" within the pharmaceutical industry. Roughly, they can be looked at as different therapeutic segments. In fact, in some of the segments there are high levels of concentration, and quite acute in some products. For example, Lupin is a dominant player in anti-tuberculosis drugs, while Cipla is dominant in anti-asthmatic drugs.

Regulations in the Pharmaceutical Industry

In a normal product market, firms can try to boost sales, and therefore profits, by reducing prices. Be that as it may, the drugs market has special characteristics. Either private or public insurance companies usually cover drug consumers in developed countries, and so they do not pay directly for medicines. Consumption patterns are not affected by prices, so firms do not have any incentive to keep prices low.

In many countries, it is the government that bears most, or all, of the costs of medicines. As a monopsonist (single buyer), the government may be able to control drug prices, and prevent drug companies from exploiting the special characteristics of the market. Nevertheless, in developing countries, the situation is quite different. People are covered neither by public nor private insurance. In the bargain, consumers are very often not the decision-makers. The doctors and the pharmacists have a significant role to play, and the companies often try to influence them, sometimes via huge incentives.

To such a degree, any regulatory mechanism for pharmaceutical products must take into account this peculiarity of the market. Hence, apart from the manufacturers, the regulatory framework must include a mechanism to regulate the behaviour of doctors, as well as the distributors of medicines, including pharmacists, at the retail level. It is precisely because of this phenomenon that, practically, all countries of the world have mechanisms to control the pharmaceuticals industry, in general, and drug prices in particular.

Pharmaceuticals Regulation In India

Till 1962, the drug industry was bereft of any price control. In 1962, in the wake of the war with China, the government feared that drug prices might rise. Accordingly, for the first time, under the Defence of India Act, 1915, statutory control was imposed on the prices of drugs and pharmaceuticals.

During 1970, the Indian Patents Act (IPA) and the Drug Prices Control Order (DPCO) were passed. Under the IPA, substances used in foods and pharmaceuticals could not be granted product patents. Only process patents were allowed for a period of five years, from date of patent grant, or seven years from date of filing for patent, whichever was earlier. The introduction of the IPA provided a major thrust to the Indian pharmaceuticals industry; and Indian companies, through the process of reverse engineering and synthesis, began to produce drugs at lower costs.

The Drugs and Cosmetics Act, 1940, governs the import, manufacture, distribution and sale of drugs in India. The Drug Controller General of India (DCGI), an authority established under the Drugs and Cosmetics Act, 1940, oversees the conduct of clinical trials. The DCGI is also responsible for the approval and registration of drugs, and it issues manufacturing and marketing licences for the same. This paper will not discuss the functioning of the DCGI, as it is beyond its scope.

The DPCO was first passed in 1970 and then revised in 1979, 1987 and 1995. In its introductory form, DPCO was a direct control on the profitability of a pharmaceutical business, and an indirect control on the prices of pharmaceuticals. The DPCO, 1979, stipulated imposing a ceiling on the prices of controlled categories of bulk drugs and their formulations. The retail prices of controlled formulations were decided by applying the concept of MAPE (Maximum Allowable Post-manufacturing Expenses).

The pricing formula was retail price= (MC+CC+PM+PC) x (1+MAPE/100) + excise duty: Where MC was the material cost, including cost of bulk drugs/excipients; CC was the conversion cost as per the dosage form; PM was the cost of packing material; and PC was the packaging charge, worked out in accordance with established costing procedures. The DPCO, 1979, put 370 drugs under price control. Through this DPCO, around 80 per cent of the Indian pharma industry (in value terms) was brought under strict price control. In the DPCO, 1987, the number of bulk drugs under price control was significantly reduced from 370 to 142.

The latest Drug Price Control Order was passed in 1995. The basic structure of this DPCO is the same as that of the earlier order, except that a uniform MAPE of 100 per cent was granted to all controlled formulations. Nevertheless, the span of price control was liberalised considerably from 142 drugs to just 76. The new Indian Pharmaceutical Policy, 2002, focused on liberalisation by reducing the number of drugs, subject to price control, and by further opening up the market to foreign investment. The new Pharmaceutical Policy, 2002, further reduced the number of drugs under price control to just 38.

Decontrol and Pharmaceutical Prices

Drugs and formulations have been subjected to price control for more than three decades now, though significant decontrol was introduced in 1995. Due to the price control and patent regime, drug prices fell, considerably in India, and were among the lowest in the world. Albeit, some studies have shown that prices of drugs started rising as soon as controls were removed.

It may no longer be true that drug prices in India are among the cheapest in the world. Drugs that are still patent-protected are much cheaper in India due to India's earlier Patent Act of 1970. But off-patent drugs (which account for 80-85 per cent of current sales in the country) are not necessarily cheaper in India. In fact, generally, drug prices are higher in India than those in Sri Lanka and Bangladesh. Even more disturbing is the fact that prices of some top selling drugs are higher in India than those in Canada and the UK.

This is so because market mechanisms are ineffective, as there is no direct interaction between the consumer and the drug market. Companies are able to sell over-priced drugs through aggressive promotional strategies, aimed at doctors, and by providing lucrative margins to pharmacies.

The pharmacy owners are also banded together to form a huge cartel, in the guise of a trade association, All India Organisation of Chemists and Druggists (AIOCD). The AIOCD launched boycotts against drug companies to win higher profit margins. AIOCD has also forced some drug companies to sign "memorandums of understanding" in which they agree to increase profit margins to pharmacies.

Major Competition Issues

Let us now take a look at the three major types of competition problems *vis-à-vis* the pharmaceutical industry in India:

- Collusions
- Mergers and acquisitions (horizontal or vertical)
- Abuse of dominance (including IPR related)

Collusions

Collusive activities among the Indian manufacturers of pharmaceuticals have not yet emerged. Still, existence of such a tendency, in certain segments where there are just a few manufacturers, cannot be ruled out. In any case, even international cartels can inflict heavy damage on Indian consumers and businesses. According to one reliable estimate, the bulk vitamins cartel alone cost India about US$25 mn in the 1990s.

Collusive behaviour of the pharmacies in India is a matter of grave concern. The benefits, of price decontrol of several drugs, are probably, going to the pharmacists disproportionately, more than the manufacturers. By giving extra profits to the pharmacist instead of reducing the retail price, the manufacturers are keeping medicine prices higher than necessary for Indian patients. This will also mean that the market for medicines will be smaller than it would have been otherwise.

As per the provisions of the new Competition Act 2002, only the trade unions are allowed to engage in collective bargaining. On that account, the activities of the pharmacists' association to extract higher margins would be illegal. Next, the law prohibits collusive behaviour, and in consequence, the association's activities would be covered by the law. Nonetheless, it is not going to be easy to take any strong action where more than 500,000 pharmacists are involved.

Mergers & Acquisitions (M&As)

As of now, the Indian pharmaceutical industry is highly fragmented. Accordingly, it is expected that the future will see intense consolidation activities. Pressure on drug prices has made global pharmaceutical Trans-national Corporations (TNCs) resort to mergers and alliances in a bid to reduce R&D duplication and costs, combine product portfolios, and increase reach so as to spread research expenditure over a larger base. The total number of alliances increased from 120 in the mid-1980s to nearly 400 in the mid-1990s. The trend is expected to continue, and such mega-mergers and alliances in the global market are likely to raise competition concerns in several markets, including India.

The new Competition Act provides for merger review beyond a threshold level. The deals will require complex analysis to examine the impact on different therapeutic segments. For example, Glaxo-Wellcome was allowed to merge with SmithKline Beecham, by the EU, on the condition that they license out product categories where competition concerns could arise. The deal went unchallenged in most developing countries. But, South Africa, who closely cooperates with the EU, imposed similar conditions before they allowed the merger. This shows how India can deal with M&A cases, not only of domestic companies but also of global companies with local presence in India. The new law in India also has extra-territorial jurisdiction, i.e. it can take action against any merger abroad, even if they don't have subsidiaries in India, but are operating here under the 'effects doctrine'.

Abuse of Dominance

Since pharmaceuticals is a knowledge-based industry, intellectual property rights play a crucial role, which mandate monopoly status to companies. Often, such monopoly status is abused to the detriment of consumers. Still, as India did not allow product patents, it was difficult for a company to sustain such a monopoly status for long. For this reason, India did not bother much about abuse of dominance in the pharmaceuticals market.

However, due to the WTO TRIPS agreement, a monopolist would essentially market all the new products, coming into the market, after the beginning of 1995. This means that in the new patent regime, abuse of dominance is likely to become quite frequent. India, then, needs to learn the art of dealing with it. The example of the Patented Medicine Prices Review Board (PMPRB) of Canada may be worth looking at, in this regard.

In Lieu of Conclusion

Pharmaceutical manufacturers are demanding more liberalisation, arguing that competition, and not price control, will improve availability and affordability of essential drugs. Even so, reducing the number of essential drugs on the DPCO will not be easy. Firstly, the United Progressive Alliance government's National Common Minimum Programme has promised to "take all steps to ensure the availability of life-saving drugs at reasonable prices". Secondly, any move to reduce the number of drugs in the DPCO may be considered to be in contravention of the Supreme Court order, on March 10, 2003 in the K.S. Gopinath case.

In any case, given the peculiarity of the market, ensuring competition is easier said than done. The Indian pharmaceutical regulatory regime has been quite hard on the manufacturers, but has been extremely soft on the two other groups of important players: the doctors and the pharmacists. Indian Medical Council (Professional Conduct, Etiquette and Ethics) Regulations, 2002 have sufficient provisions to ensure good behaviour on the part of the doctors. Be that as it may, it is more of a good endeavour rather than a binding rule. On the other hand, there is no effective monitoring or enforcement mechanism. Given the enormous clout of the pharmacists, what is badly required in India is an effective mechanism to contain the rent-seeking behaviour of the pharmacists.

The purchasers of bulk drugs are, after all, informed producers rather than helpless consumers. Like so, there is a need to study the behaviour of the bulk drug market, and, if desirable, there can be further decontrol in this regard. On the contrary, if we are talking about promoting competition in the Indian pharmaceutical market, we also need to look at import competition. Currently, except a few specified life-saving products, the duty rate is quite high. For the scheduled (regulated) drugs, the protection is much higher, as the MAPE is 100 percent for domestically manufactured drugs and 50 percent for imported drugs. The issue needs a closer look.

It is essential for the pharmaceutical sector in India to operate under a law that curbs anti-competitive activities. The new Competition Act, 2002, has all the required provisions. It would, anyhow, depend on how it is implemented.

RECOMMENDATIONS

- An effective regulatory framework is needed, which can promote good prescribing behaviour among doctors and curb collusive/rent-seeking behaviour of pharmacists.
- Mergers (including the global mega-mergers) and the IPR-related abuse of dominance are likely to raise competition concerns in coming years, and the authorities need to get their act together.
- Behaviour of the bulk drug market needs a closer look, and if desirable, there can be further decontrol in this regard.
- Except for a few specified life-saving products, the import duty rate is quite high. For the scheduled (regulated) drugs, the protection is much higher. The issue needs a closer look.

Part VI

Competition Policy in Infrastructure Sector

16

Competition Issues in Telecommunication Sector

MAHESH UPPAL*

Introduction

India's telecommunications network, which has grown to almost ten times its size in the past one decade, is one of the ten largest in the world. This network, though large, is also sparse, as even now a sixth, of the over six hundred thousand villages in the country, are still without a phone. In recent years, the sector has seen significant private sector participation, after the government's decision to liberalise and review the policy framework, and establish a regulatory body. There has been substantial growth and dramatic expansion in the range of services available, as well as a fall in their prices. The growth has been most dramatic for mobile users. Urban subscriber numbers have risen faster than rural subscribers, hinting that benefits of competition, such as choice, quality and lower prices, have not reached all, to the same extent.

Evolution of the Regulatory Framework

Till the 1980's, India's telecommunications industry was almost entirely controlled by the Government, which performed all roles including equipment manufacture, licensing, policy-making, regulations and operation of services.

With the introduction of several new electronic communications services in the early 90's, the Government took the view, in 1992, that the new "value-added services" could be left for private sector entrepreneurs to provide. Rather unusually, cellular mobile services,

* Director, Telecommunications & Computer Information Systems, New Delhi

which require significant infrastructure, like towers, to be built, were classified as value added services. In effect, the opening, in 1992, of cellular services, to private sector operators, heralded the beginning of network creation by private entrepreneurs. The entry of the private sector in other telecommunications services was finally cleared, in May 1994, when the National Telecom Policy (NTP) was announced.

NTP-94 outlined the basic policy framework for the development of the telecommunication sector in the country. It allowed private sector, including foreign, companies, to provide all services; and referred to the large investment (Rs 230 bn) required to meet the telephony targets, detailed in the policy, as the main reason to invite private sector participation. Interestingly, there was no acknowledgement *per se* of the benefits of, or need for, competition in bringing down prices, improving quality, or market expansion.

With the entry of private sector players in the cellular market, India's telecom sector, for the first time, experienced competition in the provision of telecom services. The Telecom Regulatory Authority of India (TRAI) was set up in 1997; well after mobile services had begun in 1995.

The Government players, Mahanagar Telephone Nigam Ltd. (MTNL) and Department of Telecommunications (DoT), initially opted out of the mobile market. It was felt that fixed line demand needed to be addressed first, and that highly priced mobile services had a little role in a poor country like India.

With the rapid growth world wide of mobile telephones, DoT and MTNL realised that they had probably erred in choosing to stay out of the lucrative mobile market, and attempted to play spoil sport. The DoT hiked the tariff for calls from fixed lines to mobiles, making it more expensive for people to call mobiles from fixed lines. Soon after MTNL announced plans to enter the mobile market.

Mobile operators approached the newly created TRAI, which quashed the DoT tariff proposals as well as disallowed MTNL from entering the mobile market. This was on the grounds that the terms and conditions of MTNL's licences were unavailable, and the Government had not sought its prior approval when it licensed MTNL to provide mobile services. TRAI also sought to move the mobile operators to calling-party-pays regime, where the mobile user, like the fixed one, would pay only to make outgoing calls. However, the DoT appealed to the High Court against these decisions of TRAI and won.

Consequently, TRAI's role in licensing was reduced, as the Government did not need to consult it on any licensing decisions. TRAI also did not have the power to alter revenue sharing arrangements i.e. the interconnection terms of operators.

The private businesses soon found themselves in financial trouble and unable to pay the huge amounts committed in licence fees. This resulted in defaults, and disputes between operators and DoT - as to who was responsible for the failure of new operators to pay their dues. The High Court ruled against the operators when they sought to prevent Government from taking action against defaulters and encashing guarantees given by operators. The private operators lost all their cases. They felt that the regulatory regime did not provide sufficient incentive or security to new investors. This was particularly worrying since the Government was compromised, because of the obvious conflict of interest, in its roles as licensor, policy maker, regulator and operator.

Faced with the dilemma, of allowing the private operators to die out and face the resulting bad publicity, or changing its approach, the government chose the latter. It announced a change in policy through the formulation of the New Telecom Policy 1999. From the operators' perspective, the most important part of the NTP-99 proposals, was the move from a licence fee regime to a revenue sharing regime, and permission for DoT and MTNL to enter the mobile business. Importantly, NTP-99 differed in its focus, in that now the creation of a competitive telecommunications sector was recognised as an objective, as was the need for a level playing field.

NTP-99 was followed, in 2000, by the amendment of TRAI Act (1997). The amendment gave TRAI the exclusive mandate to fix and regulate tariffs, and interconnection; and removed all Government say in these two functions. It also mandated the Government to seek advice from TRAI before it licensed a new operator, although such advice would not be binding. The amendment envisaged reconstitution of the TRAI, and the creation, in addition, of the Telecom Dispute Settlement and Appellate Tribunal – to which inter-operator disputes, operator-government disputes, and appeals against

TRAI's decisions could be made. However, in the new dispensation, the TRAI members enjoyed no legal protection, beyond a right of being heard, if the Government wished to remove them from office.

The operating company, Bharat Sanchar Nigam Limited (BSNL), was carved out of the DoT in 2000, leaving a smaller DoT to deal with policy making and related government functions, including licensing and spectrum management.

Unified Licensing Regime

With technological advances, it was realised that the CDMA technology, which was being used by fixed line players, could also be used to provide mobile telephony. Consequently, limited mobility services began in 2002; much to the displeasure of the GSM based mobile operators. The result was aggressive litigation by cellular mobile service providers, who alleged foul play and back door entry into their mobile business for which they had paid huge licence fees.

To put an end to the controversy, the TRAI made a proposal to the Government to merge or unify fixed and mobile licences, which was readily accepted. This was the first step towards a unified licensing regime. As a final step towards unification, TRAI released its draft recommendations on the Unified Licensing Regime, in August 2004. However, instead of using it as an opportunity to address all anomalies in the system and encourage growth of new technologies, TRAI has chosen to protect existing long-distance operators, and postpone the use of new technology for another five years. Till the time of writing this brief, the recommendations remain to be finalised.

Market Structure in Telecommunications

The competitive pressure, following the entry of two more mobile players in 2001, led to a considerable fall in prices and expansion of services. However, there is limited competition in the fixed line business, as BSNL and MTNL between them control almost 95 per cent of the fixed line subscribers. Private sector companies, Reliance, and Bharti, lead the market shares in the mobile business with BSNL, a close third.

Competition, in the long distance market, has led to a over 75 per cent fall in long distance rates, both nationally and internationally. The Internet market, too, has begun to show the fixed line incumbents as the likely winners. Starting from scratch, today, they are ahead of operators such as Sify and VSNL, who started services long before BSNL or MTNL.

Changes in the regulatory regime and the policy environment have led to consolidation in the Indian telecommunications sector. Post NTP-99, when the operators were freed from huge licence fee commitments, the market saw the exit of several small companies. The M&A activity got a further boost with the unification of the fixed and mobile licences in the country.

In the case of fixed line services, which are still the mainstay of most rural consumers, the situation is problematic. In most cases, only one operator, BSNL, serves rural areas. Most rural consumers in India still do not have access to competition, and its consequent benefits through more attractive prices, quality as well as actual choice. Indeed, it is seen that consuming subscribers are fewer in the semi-urban and rural regions, and they pay higher call charges.

Existence of Anti-competitive Practices

The rapid growth in the telecommunications sector, in recent years tempts one to view the progress as a consequence of increasing competition. This is unfortunately true, to a limited extent only. The sector is currently witnessing a considerable range of anti-competitive practices. It is also ironic that several of these practices emanate from, or concern, the Government-owned BSNL because of the Government's role in licensing, policy-making and operations.

The most brazen anti-competitive practice in the market, today, is that BSNL (along with MTNL which operates in Delhi and Mumbai) operates an integrated service for the whole of India, while its competitors are licensed for each region and service separately. The latter's licences came on payment of substantial fees in most cases. BSNL has not paid a licence fee to provide any service. Thus Bharti, Reliance, BPL, Hutch, etc have obtained separate licences to serve different states, after the payment of fees. The private sector, therefore, has an inherent disadvantage when it competes with BSNL.

Furthermore, even after the unification of fixed and mobile licences, a licensee, who holds licences for contiguous areas, is required to reach its customers, in the other area, only by connecting to long distance service providers, amongst which BSNL is the most ubiquitous and largest.

Regulations, today, allow BSNL to receive an Access Deficit Charge (ADC), which seeks to compensate BSNL, whose fixed line rentals and call charges are considered loss-making operations that must be continued in public interest. Importantly, operators of mobile services pay ADC, even if the calls themselves do not reach the fixed network at all. As things stand, against all norms of fair competition, BSNL receives ADC payments from its competitors, even though it refuses to undertake tariff revision that current TRAI regulations have allowed it to carry out for several years. The perverse incentive for BSNL to adopt this approach is easy to see, since the losses so incurred can be directly recovered from payments from its competitors. There is no transparency in the use of ADC amount, as BSNL has not effected account separation to justify the amount it is receiving.

Among other competition concerns are BSNL's refusal to share its infrastructure with its competitors, even though regulations demand it. BSNL is yet to come up with its Reference Interconnect Offer, mandated by TRAI, while it has frequently threatened to cancel interconnection agreements if competitors do not accept its term and conditions, in their totality.

A phenomenon which has now acquired considerable importance, is the fact that BSNL has now become India's largest Internet Service Operator (ISP), even though it was one of the last companies to enter the business. A closer look at the picture demonstrates that unlike its competitors, who have usually one business i.e. of ISP, BSNL has two when it comes to Internet services. BSNL provides dialup access to the public telephony network, that its own users as well as most of the customers of its competitors need, and the ISPs (e.g. Sify) cannot provide. This anomaly gives BSNL two revenue streams *viz*, call charges for access to the telephone network, and charges for providing Internet access. The opportunity for cross-subsidising the competitive ISP business, with the less competitive dial-up business, is obvious.

BSNL has also successfully thwarted the attempts of competing ISPs, by making it difficult to access the net through use of competing network providers (e.g. Bharti), who would have an incentive to offer more attractive pricing to ISPs.

Relationship and Coordination Between Regulatory Agencies

The biggest threat to competition, in the telecommunication market today, is the distortions in the market caused by government policy, rules and regulation, set by different government agencies. There are two levels at which coordination is necessary. One is between the TRAI and the Competition Commission of India (CCI). The other is between TRAI and the Wireless Planning Co-ordination (WPC) wing.

In the context of dealing with competition issues, there may be a risk of "forum shopping" in the two agencies: TRAI and CCI, with an overlapping mandate, since it might be an incentive for people to approach agencies, which seem to them to be likely to promise their kind of relief. This requires establishing a mechanism for continuous coordination between the two agencies. The case of South Africa is interesting: The Competition Commission and the Independent Communication Authority of South Africa (ICASA) have entered into a memorandum of agreement, under which both bodies can act, pursuant to their authorising statutes, while allocating a lead role to one or the other in a particular case.

The coordination between TRAI and WPC is also critical in the new environment, where wireless communication is increasingly the most convenient and inexpensive method of connecting people and places.

Finally, the issue of the Communications Convergence Bill, which is pending before the parliament: The Communications Convergence Bill seeks to bring all communication services under one regulatory framework, but is pending among mild controversies. For example, broadcasting, cable TV, media, etc. In the USA, there is one super regulator: Federal Communications Commission, which deals with all such services under one framework. In India, a similar approach, by bringing the Communication Convergence Bill to fruition, will be very helpful.

RECOMMENDATIONS

- Make TRAI independent of government funding and control
- Expand TRAI's staff strength and provide capacity building
- Ensure transparent accounting by BSNL, to create a true level playing field
- Establish clear norms and a hierarchy for TRAI, and the competition authority, with respect to their roles in addressing competition issues in telecommunications

17

Competition and Regulation in Energy Sector in India

DEVENDRA KODWANI*

Introduction

Efficiency of the energy sector has a cascading effect on the overall socio-economic development. In the year 2001, India accounted for 3.5 per cent of the commercial energy demand of the world, which is the sixth highest consumption in the world. With an annual GDP growth rate target of 8 per cent for the future, the energy demand is expected to grow at 5.2 per cent. Even though, per capita consumption of energy at 479 kg of oil equivalent (kgoe) is just one-fifth of the world average. The Planning Commission of India estimates that the energy demand is likely to grow at 6.6 per cent and 6.1 per cent respectively during the 10th and the 11th Five Year plans.

Catching up with this demand would need fresh investments for the efficient exploitation of primary energy sources like coal, oil and natural gas, and non-fossil fuel based power generation. Productivity of the primary energy sectors (including coal, oil/natural gas) as well as secondary (such as electricity generation, supply and distribution) is also a concern.

The coal sector in India was nationalised through the Coal Mines (Nationalisation) Act, 1973. In the year 1976, captive mining was allowed by the private sector producing iron and steel, and also to sub-lease mining where rail transportation was not required. The Act was further amended, in the year 1993, to allow captive mining by the private sector for power generation, and value-addition in terms of washing of coal, and to cement producers at a later stage. In the year 2000, the Coal India (Regulation of

---

* Director, Tolani Institute of Management, Kutch, Gujarat

Transfers and Validation) Act was passed to empower the Central Government to direct the transfer, or allocation of property, and mining rights through Coal India Ltd. or any other subsidiary company.

Table 17.1

Estimated Energy Demand for India

Primary Fuel	*Unit*	*Demand (in original units)*		*Demand (MTOE)*	
		2006-07	*2011-12*	*2006-07*	*2011-12*
Coal	Mt	460.50	620.00	190.00	254.93
Lignite	Mt	57.79	81.54	15.51	22.05
Oil	Mt	134.50	172.47	144.58	185.40
Natural Gas	BCM	47.45	64.00	42.70	57.60
Hydro Power	BKwh	148.08	215.66	12.73	18.54
Nuclear Power	BKwh	23.15	54.75	6.04	14.16
Wind Power	BKwh	4.00	11.62	0.35	1.00
Total Commercial Energy			411.91	553.68	
Non-Commercial Energy			151.30	170.25	
Total Energy Demand			**563.21**	**723.93**	

Note: MTOE: Million Tonnes Oil Equivalent; Mt: Million Tonnes; BCM: Billion Cubic Meter; Bkwh: Billion kilo watt hours.

Source: 10th Five Year Plan Document, Planning Commission, Govt. of India

At present, only consuming public sector units are allowed to mine coal for non-captive purposes. The attempts made by the Government, to introduce the private sector to non-captive mining, have not succeeded for several reasons. As of January 2001, coal reserves for the country are estimated to be 220.98 billion tonnes (bt). Out of this, proven reserves are at 84.41 bt, while 98.55 bt are indicated reserves, and 38.02 bt are inferred reserves.

Hydrocarbons (oil and natural) contribute approximately 45 per cent (nearly 36 per cent from oil and 9 per cent from natural gas) to India's total energy supply. In the year 2001-02, demand for petroleum products was 100.43 million tonnes (MnT), witnessing a growth of about 4.9 per cent during the period 1997-2002. Successful exploration and efficient refining, and logistics, determine the overall cost of this primary source of energy. Before the nationalisation of oil companies, the oil markets were dominated by multinationals. Currently, the sector is dominated by government enterprises, though the private sector has made a dent.

The average per capita, consumption of electricity in India has nearly doubled in the last twenty years. From a per capita consumption of 178 Kwhs in 1985, it has reached 355 Kwhs in the year 2000. Almost all electricity generation, transmission and distribution, is managed by the public sector, i.e. State Electricity Boards and Central Utilities. There are few private sector companies in electricity supply in Kolkata, Mumbai, Ahmedabad, New Delhi, etc. Prior to the enactment of the Electricity Act, 2003, three legislations, namely the Indian Electricity Act, 1910, the Electricity Supply Act, 1948, and the Central Regulatory Act, 1998 were governing the sector.

Nature of the Industry

At present, the market structure for coal production and distribution in India, is completely dominated by the State owned entities, with nearly 85 per cent of the total production coming from the collieries of Coal India Ltd, and its subsidiaries. About 10 per cent supply comes from another public sector enterprise, Singareni Collieries Company Limited (SCCL).

The coal supply has increased from 70 mnt per annum, at the time of nationalisation, to 355 mnt in 2003-04. In addition to indigenous supply, various consumers also import coal, since it is freely importable (being in Open General List), with an import duty ranging from 5 to 15 per cent for different grades.

In the year 2000, deregulation occurred, leaving no authority to the Central Government to fix the prices. Yet, effective competition around differential pricing is unlikely to arise, as almost the entire supply side in the non-captive segment is dominated by public enterprises, that too by a single supplier.

Distribution of coal is still managed or mediated through government agencies. Allocation to core sectors (defined by the Government for this purpose, to include Power, Steel, Cement, Defence, Fertiliser and Railways) is done through two committees of the Ministry of Coal. Nonetheless, in the emerging new policy framework, for coal sales to the non-core sector, stress is being given on bilateral agreements between supplying subsidiary companies and consumers, for well-defined commitment on the part of both buyers and sellers.

Legislative clearance for the introduction of the private sector, in coal mining and marketing, is the biggest hurdle to be faced in India as the first step to introduce competition in this sector. Since coal contributes to nearly 50 per cent of the total indigenous primary energy supply in India, it would be desirable that the full potential of this sector is harnessed through competitive forces and private entrepreneurs. The reasons include that, it being a labour-intensive industry, trade unions are likely to wield a lot of power with their strong political affiliations. There have been several attempts on the part of the Government to discuss the matter with trade unions, but so far the proposed bill to reform the sector has not been presented in the Parliament.

Based upon the recommendations of a policy group of the Government on Hydrocarbon Vision–2025, oil PSUs were restructured for competitiveness. The state owned PSUs were consolidated in the year 2001, through mergers and buyouts, to make them stronger and capable to withstand the likely increase in competition. Looking at global market trends, few large corporations are emerging in oligopolistic competition. Therefore, the consolidation is expected to strengthen the competitive position of PSUs, as economies of scale in refining and distribution would reduce the operating costs.

The New Exploration Licensing Policy (NELP) provides incentives, and a level playing field, to private parties who could bid for exploration blocks. Such measures have created an incentive, for private sector enterprises, to bring capital into high-risk exploration activity and capital incentive refineries.

One major reform in the sector has been the abolition of the Administrative Price Mechanism (APM) with effect from 31 March 2002. This step must go a long way in both demand and supply management. This, anyhow, is not complete freedom to fix the price. Rather, the revision is to be discussed with the Government, each time. On the other hand, the thorny issue of subsidies on kerosene and liquefied petroleum gas (LPG) would still need to be resolved. Oil companies have been arguing for the Government to subsidise the target beneficiary population directly, rather than through them. The situation can be compared with electricity supplies to agriculture and domestic consumers.

A significant step, towards introducing competition at the downstream value chain, was to de-canalise kerosene oil, low sulphur diesel and LPG. From 1993 onwards, private players are allowed to import and market these products, at market-determined prices in parallel to the marketing system, which is dominated by PSUs. The parallel suppliers are not required to obtain any approval, from the Ministry of Petroleum & Natural Gas, for undertaking the parallel marketing of these products. Though the volume of fuel imported for the parallel marketing system is not huge, this has introduced competition in the distribution segment of the petroleum sector, to a limited extent.

Since the year 1991, the Government has been trying to restructure and divest its stake in oil companies, but employees and political parties have resisted the move. Notwithstanding this, Government control of Indian Petrochemical Corporation Ltd. was taken over by Reliance Industries, and part of the government ownership was transferred to individuals through a public offer. Given the absence of political consensus, the privatisation of oil companies looks unlikely in the near future.

The Power sector in India is in the Concurrent List of the Constitution, which means the Central government as well as the State governments are both empowered to engage in the generation and supply of power. Although there have been policy initiatives since the early nineties to encourage the private sector, success so far has been far from satisfactory.

The Ninth Plan envisaged an addition of 40245.2 MW generation capacity, but the actual capacity addition is less than half. The state sector was to add 22656.7 MW, against which it managed to add only 13954.1 MW. The real disappointment, and failure, of policy reform was attracting private investment with just 5061 MWs addition against the expected 17588.5 MWs. In the year 2002, total private generation capacity stood at 10 per cent, with the rest owned and managed by state suppliers. Thermal and hydro-based plants contribute nearly 85 per cent of installed capacity, while gas based plants account for 10 per cent. Other plants use diesel, wind and nuclear power as fuel.

Suboptimal investment in transmission and distribution over the years, compared to generation, is resulting in operational inefficiency and high losses. The financial performance of State Electricity Boards (SEBs) has been very poor. Price distortions are acute. The tariff for the agricultural sector recovers barely 15 per cent of the cost of supply in some states. SEBs have been incurring operating losses (commercial losses), which were estimated to be Rs. 24837.22 crore in 2001-02. The amount of unrecovered subsidies has been increased, to push SEBs to financial sickness, with negative rates of returns ranging from 12 per cent to 40 per cent. Emergence of competitive market structures would require these issues to be addressed upfront.

Competition Concerns

To create competition in the coal sector, private enterprises should be allowed to carry out mining for non-captive purposes and compete with the government-owned coal suppliers. This can only be done when marketing and distribution is freed from government control and allocations. Administered allocation to core and non-core sectors has made it possible for some of the users of coal, particularly the SEBs, to get their supplies, despite being quite poor in paying up the dues. Regulated allocation also limits price competition, as allocation is not guided by price bids, but other considerations. Another policy measure that facilitates competition in the coal sector is the restructuring of Coal India Ltd. and making the subsidiaries of CIL independent companies, which could be first corporatised, and then privatised. The scope of economic regulation in the coal sector is negligible; hence both prices and investments should be left to the market.

Government control over the retail prices of petroleum products is a hurdle in the way of introducing competition. The proposed Petroleum Regulatory Board Bill needs to be debated extensively, prior to it becoming a law. Exploration, development, and refining do not require economic regulation, as they have potential to become competitive. But, at the retail level, the issue of subsidised delivery mechanisms needs to be sorted out appropriately. Common carriage for oil and gas offers the case where economic regulation is required.

Vertically integrated State Electricity Boards dominate the industry so far, as they generate, transmit, supply and distribute. Though the Electricity Act (2003) has mandated State Governments to unbundle the SEBs, simple restructuring would not simplify the competition and regulation issues. Though, open access has been promised, interstate transmission and distribution within states is still a monopoly.

The Electricity Act provides the required policy framework for increased private participation. Although, private enterprises will set up the generation plants only if the thorny issue of transmission tariff fixation is resolved satisfactorily. Transmission of electricity shows signs of natural monopoly, where competition appears unlikely. That would necessitate economic regulation to secure economic efficiency.

Generation constitutes around 60-65 per cent of the total cost of the electricity supply, about 10 per cent is the transmission cost, and remaining 25 per cent or so accounts for distribution. Hence, effective competition in the generation segment can substantially improve the efficiency, and result in lower cost, of the electricity supply. But distribution companies, currently being largely inefficient, provide substantial scope in efficiency improvements. The Act provides for a second licence for distribution, but it is more important to expose the distribution companies to pressures of markets, namely to decisions of both consumers and investors. This can only be achieved when open access is provided on workable terms.

Subsidies pose the greatest political hurdle in the creation of real competition in the distribution segment, which, in turn, affects the emergence of a credible market, even in generation. A diffused, non-targeted, non-merit based subsidy delivery mechanism, is one of the biggest hurdles in the way of privatisation of distribution entities. Tackled successfully, it is feasible, economically and technically, to introduce competition in the distribution segment.

In case of mergers and takeovers in the generation sector, transferability of property rights is crucial. The overlap of jurisdiction of the Competition Commission, and sectoral regulators, is an enigma. The Competition Commission is not empowered to adjudicate, while the Central Electricity Regulatory Commission (CERC) is. Issues related to competition between generating companies, or other anticompetitive behaviour, that impacts upon the competitive working of generating companies are not touched upon. The Electricity Act envisages the CERC and State Electricity Regulatory Commissions (SERCs) to promote competition in the electricity sector. Nevertheless, the duties of regulatory and competition authorities are likely to overlap in this regard.

Having an apex regulatory body for the entire energy sector is advisable, rather than separate regulators for each sector, since economics of related network industries, like gas and electricity distribution, would lead to convergence of these industries. Nonetheless, everyone is not actually convinced about this suggestion.

Conclusions

In India, Government still dominates most of the primary as well as secondary energy sectors, at large, though a beginning has been made to allow the private sector into the area.

Judging by its vital role in overall economic growth, the energy sector needs to be looked at, comprehensively, with a holistic approach. Arriving at the right mix of energy sources is crucial. Competitiveness, just within a sector would not be sufficient, rather it is desirable to explore as to what extent the primary energy industries can compete with each other as well. This needs to be studied further.

The issues of regulation and competition policy are complex in the energy sector. Any piecemeal approach to policy formulation or implementation would delay the development of competitive markets. A cohesive view of competition, in the entire energy sector, is missing so far. Recently there were reports that the Government is working towards developing a comprehensive energy policy. In that case, it would be interesting to observe how much importance is given to make the sector competitive.

It is advisable that keeping the bigger picture in mind, the choice between economic regulation *versus* competition be examined very carefully. Such considerations are required even within a sector. For instance, the scope of economic regulation is limited in oil exploration, development, refining and value addition, and retail markets. However, transmission through common carriage, or transportation of crude and processed oil, needs to be regulated. Therefore, before the proposed Petroleum Regulatory Board Bill becomes a law, it needs to be debated extensively. Broadly, the petroleum sector requires a comprehensive competitive framework rather than stringent regulations.

To make the coal sector competitive, allowing private players for non-captive mining seems the next logical step, followed by divesting the government-owned corporations. The petroleum sector has witnessed gradual reforms – the steps taken so far have been in the direction of creating more market-based decisions by producers and users. Even so, two major decisions on the complete deregulation of retail pricing of petroleum products, and privatisation of oil PSUs, remain to be taken.

The most significant changes have been introduced in the power sector. There has been a sustained attempt at designing an appropriate policy, to create competitive markets in the electricity supply chain. Yet, much remains to be done, particularly about the tricky issues of subsidised supplies to certain consumers. Looking at the complexity and political significance of the sector, it has become difficult to proceed, for most of the states, towards meaningful restructuring of the markets in the electricity supply. The Electricity Act (2003) has proposed sea changes in the way electricity markets could be reformed. Still, any effective change will take time, and painstaking efforts will be required to push forward the reform agenda towards creation of competitive markets.

RECOMMENDATIONS

- Study the varied international experiences, and frame the sectoral competition policy for the energy sector in India.
- Gather global experiences, and examine the possibility for having an integrated regulatory regime for primary as well as secondary energy industry in India.
- Estimate the potential economic gains of the energy industry, in India, becoming competitive.
- Assessment of the impact of intra-sector, as well as inter-sectoral, M&As in the Indian energy industry, and their impact on competition.
- Calculate the likely impact of 'Open Access' to transmission and distribution infrastructure, on the competitiveness of the electricity sector.

18

Competition Issues in Transportation Sectors

SUNIL JAIN*

Introduction

While the transport sector has grown at a healthy rate of 10 percent a year, during the last decade (12 per cent for roadways, 1.4 for railways and 8.0 for seaports and air ports), this is the sector that has the greatest possibility to hold back India's GDP growth target of eight per cent.

For instance, the Rakesh Mohan Committee Report on Infrastructure (1996) estimated the economic losses from bad roads at anywhere up to Rs 30,000 crore a year, or around 1 to 2 per cent of GDP each year.

Since the early 1990s, the Government has made efforts to fix things. In just the last decade, the share of minor ports, many of them new ones, developed by the private sector, is up from around 6 per cent to 25 per cent in total ports traffic. The private sector has been allowed to create capacity in major ports as well. Similarly, repealing the Air Corporation Act of 1953 and replacing this with a new law in 1994, that allowed competition, and private participation in the scheduled domestic air transport services, led to a dramatic surge in traffic.

Yet, the transport sector remains very inefficient. While airport charges in India are, on an average, 80 per cent higher than the international average, air travel in India costs a lot more. In the case of seaports, while Indian ports charge less than global rates for cargo-related services, the vessel-related charges are four times higher, as a result of which the total costs in India are around a sixth higher.

---

* Contributing Editor, Business Standard, New Delhi

The reason for this sorry state of affairs eventually boils down to policies that inhibit competition in the sectors, and poor regulation.

In the case of the ports sector, for instance, despite allowing the private sector to invest in major ports, there are few instances of this happening, as it is up to the port authority (the Government) to decide to allow competition. It is worse in the case of the railways. They are the primary medium for transporting containers across the country's vast hinterland and enjoy a total monopoly over this, through the Container Corporation of India (Concor). In the aviation sector, similarly, the Government has just allowed private airlines to fly abroad, but the barriers to entry are still high, and all types of levies are put on aviation fuel. Goods transport by road is often at the mercy of cartels of transport firms, who dictate freight rates.

Civil Aviation

Most airports in the country are owned by the Government and managed by the Airport Authority of India (AAI). In India, though the number of airports is more than in some of the neighbouring countries, like China, most are underutilised and underdeveloped. Presently, various airlines are operating only through 61 airports. The remaining are lying unused – handling, at best, occasional aircraft operations. Even though airport charges are among the highest in the world, only ten airports in the country make profits. The others remain poorly equipped, with mounting losses.

In 1953, consequent to the coming into force of the Air Corporations Act (1953), the Government nationalised the airline industry. In accordance with this Act, the two air corporations, *viz*, Indian Airlines Corporation and Air India International, were established and the assets of all the then existing air companies (nine) were transferred to the two new Corporations. The operation of scheduled air transport services was made a monopoly of these two Corporations.

In 1994, the wheel turned a full circle as the Air Corporations Act (1953) was repealed with effect from March 1994. With that, the monopoly of the Corporations on scheduled air transport services ended. The repeal of the Air Corporations Act has enabled private operators to provide scheduled air transport services.

The government-owned Indian Airlines, and the private operators, Jet Airways and Air Sahara, provide regular domestic services. Air

Deccan, 'a low-cost, no-frills carrier' has recently started operations. Air India – the national carrier–carries domestic travellers between metro cities, from where it operates international flights. Indian Airlines also flies to a few international destinations in the neighbouring countries in South Asia, as well as to the Gulf.

The entry of domestic private airlines to international destinations has been allowed in early 2004, and was first restricted to the SAARC region. Very recently, the Government has allowed domestic private airlines to fly to international destinations, except the Gulf region.

With the entry of private operators, competition has increased. There has been an improvement in the quality of services. Airlines are cutting fares and offering other 'freebies' to expand their market share. On some domestic routes, the fares are now even lower than what they were ten years ago. With the entry of 'no-frills' airlines, competition in the civil aviation sector has entered a new phase.

Till a couple of years back, the public sector Indian Airlines, being the dominant player, enjoyed a market share of over 60 per cent and set the trend – be it in additional services, discounted fares or special rates and incentives. But now, with new players coming into the market, the situation has changed. Air Sahara and Jet Airways often take the lead in special packages. Now, it is the turn of Air Deccan to come up with new schemes, such as dynamic fares.

Furthermore, till 2003, the fare war among the domestic airlines, especially Indian Airlines, Jet and Sahara, was on domestic flights. Now, with the opening of international routes to private operators, the competition is also spreading to international routes.

Presently, the Airports Authority of India (AAI) is responsible for regulating and operating airports, and providing air traffic services. These multiple roles obviously create serious conflicts of interest.

The Naresh Chandra Committee on Civil Aviation has recommended unbundling of the AAI, along with corporatisation of airport management. The committee has suggested that each of the larger airports should be managed by an independent corporate entity, while the smaller airports could be grouped together on a regional basis and corporatised. This would help these secondary airports to get the attention they deserve.

The unbundling of AAI would ensure that conflicting functions, most importantly the regulatory function, are hived off to independent entities. Among other things, an independent regulator is needed to keep a watch on pricing, because airport services are usually a monopoly.

Given these recommendations, the Cabinet Committee on Infrastructure has recently decided to establish a regulator for the civil aviation sector. The regulator will be concerned with all economic activities, including landing, tariff, freight and user charges. The proposed regulator will be different from the Director General of Civil Aviation (DGCA), who will only look after air traffic control, security and safety.

The Government is also planning to allow private players to supply aviation turbine fuel (ATF), which is currently a monopoly of the state-owned firms. The ATF is one of the major operating costs of airlines in the country, accounting for about 30 per cent of the total operating costs, as opposed to the global level of about 15 per cent. The entry of private operators, and the consequent competition in the supply of ATF in the country, is expected to reduce the costs. This would lead to further reduction in airfares, which are presently constrained by costs, such as ATF, on which the airlines do not have any control.

Competition Concerns in Civil Aviation

Despite the various initiatives taken by the Government of India, and the various initiatives it plans to undertake, there are certain concerns relating to competition in the civil aviation sector.

One of them relates to the level playing field concerning the state-owned carriers. Civil aviation is a sector where government intervention has affected the competitiveness of state-owned carriers, and their ability to compete effectively with the private operators.

The civil aviation policy, for instance, insists that all scheduled carriers fly at least 10 per cent of their capacity, on trunk routes, in the north-eastern sector, Jammu & Kashmir, Andaman & Nicobar Islands and Lakshadweep (category-II routes). Since load factors in this region are poor, it is a loss-making proposition. Due to political pressures, the state-owned carrier, Indian Airlines (IA), is forced to fly 17 per cent of its flights on these routes, and incurs an extra annual loss of Rs 62 crore due to this. What this does, of course, is to lower Indian Airlines' competitiveness and restricts inter-airline competition.

In addition, the law states that 50 per cent of trunk route flights have to be flown on Category III routes (that is, on non-trunk and non-category-II routes). On these routes too, IA is forced to fly a greater share of flights in comparison with private airlines. According to figures provided by airline officials, IA flies 74 per cent of flights, servicing these smaller towns, and loses Rs 134 crore a year on this.

As if this was not enough, the procedural bottlenecks in the Government, hamper investment in aircraft by the public sector airlines. For the past three years, the public sector airlines have been trying to procure aircrafts to expand their fleet. Unfortunately, their proposals are still doing the rounds of the government departments in search for a final approval.

The delay over aircraft acquisition has resulted in foreign airlines utilising 70 per cent of their entitlements, whereas Indian carriers are utilising only 30 per cent. It has been suggested that the private airlines be allowed to use the bilateral traffic rights which are not utilised by the public sector carriers.

Unfortunately, the argument is not as simple as allocating unused bilateral traffic rights to private airlines. Had the state-owned airlines been allowed to acquire more aircrafts, there would have been no unused bilaterals in the first place. The state-owned airlines appear to be deliberately suppressed to allow the private sector to consolidate.

There is clearly a need to establish a fair playing field, and a policy, on the role of the public sector airlines. Instead of ad-hoc allocation, a clear policy is needed on the distribution of bilaterals between the public carriers and the various private airlines, existing and forthcoming. This may be done by way of competitive bidding.

With the opening up of the skies, full autonomy needs to be given to the public sector airlines so that they can take on the competition. Top managers of the public sector airlines say that there is no dearth of ideas, or plans, to chart out a course of action, but it involves government clearance at every stage.

On the flip side, in the airports, like in Delhi or Mumbai, for instance, the state-owned Indian Airlines has a full terminal to itself, while the private-sector competitors are all cramped into one. This is despite the fact that Jet Airways, alone, has a higher market share than Indian Airlines. This has been possible because the government-run Airports Authority of India controls all terminals, and only Indian Airlines is allowed to provide third-party ground-handling services.

Due to state taxes and charges on fuel, airlines flying in India pay around 75-80 per cent more for having to buy fuel in the country. Apart from lowering the viability of airlines, this also impacts inter-airline competition, as any airline that is able to fly overseas, and pick up fuel there, is better placed. This explains the rush by private airlines to fly abroad.

The Government's recent announcement to allow only experienced (5 years' operation), private sector airlines to fly to foreign destinations will restrict the entry of other less-experienced operators, mainly the no-frills airlines, for a certain period. This would, in turn, limit competition on international routes. It is not surprising that the two beneficiaries, Jet Airways and Air Sahara, had made this demand a few months ago. While, on one hand, the two airlines have been pleading with the Government to allow them to fly to all overseas destinations (till now the exclusive preserve of state-owned airlines), on the other hand, they have been demanding for such restrictive provisions.

Ports

There are 12 major ports and 185 minor/intermediate ports in the country. Indian ports are the gateways to India's international trade by sea, and are handling over 90 per cent of foreign trade.

The major ports, which are managed by the Port Trust of India, under Central Government jurisdiction, handle about 76 per cent traffic, and thus bear the brunt of sea-borne trade.

The minor ports, which are under the jurisdiction of the respective State Governments, constitute an important, competitive alternative to the major ports. Cargo handling operations are undertaken in about 61 ports while the remaining are restricted to fishing and passenger traffic. The latter half of the 1990's witnessed the emergence of these minor ports as major players in cargo handling. Their share in maritime traffic has gone up from 10 per cent in 1996-97 to 24 per cent in 2003-04.

In keeping with the general policy of economic liberalisation, the port sector has been thrown open to private sector participation. A number of existing facilities have been taken over by private players, and many new facilities have also been set up at existing ports. Five container terminals have been handed over to private parties in the last five years. Two new ports (Mundra and Pipavav in Gujarat) have also been constructed in the private sector.

Private sector participation in operations, and infrastructure activities, of seaports has resulted in a radical change in the organisational model of ports, converting from a service port model to a landlord port model, where the port authority retains the port infrastructure and regulatory functions, and private operators provide the port services. With privatisation, the role of Indian ports, too, is changing from a service port model to a landlord port model. Ennore Port is one such example.

P&O (Peninsular & Oriental) Ports of Australia, and Port of Singapore Authority International (PSA International) are among the largest investors in the port sector in India. P&O received the first container terminal (at Jawaharlal Nehru Port) in the country to be offered to private participation. The project is called the Nhava Sheva International Container Terminal.

The Tariff Authority for Major Ports (TAMP), an independent authority, has also been set up, but its authority is limited only to the determination of tariffs at major ports. It does not have any authority to take other measures to introduce competition, such as the telecom and electricity regulators have.

While there has been a fairly dramatic turnaround in Indian ports, and the average turnaround time for vessels in India's ports has improved from 8.1 days in 1990-91 to 3.7 in 2001-02, this is still very high compared to just a few hours, in ports like Colombo. What makes things worse is that, except for the Jawaharlal Nehru Port Trust (JNPT) (where there are already two operators and a third has recently been introduced), handling costs have gone up by around 15 per cent, on an average, in the period 1995-96 to 2001-02 – this at a time when India's costs are already higher than those in other countries.

In the few ports where there has been some competition, like the JNPT, the difference is discernible. The P&O Australia run Nhava

Sheva Terminal's productivity levels are at least two-thirds higher than those of JNPT, and not surprisingly its turnaround time is also around a third less, and traffic volumes around two-thirds more.

The Government has also taken measures, in recent years, to allow major ports to compete with private and minor ports. Till very recently, the Tariff Authority for Major Ports (TAMP) used to set floor prices, below which the ports were not allowed to compete. Now, the Government has asked TAMP to begin considering putting ceiling prices instead.

Competition Concerns in Ports

In terms of technical parameters, the rate of progress in India's ports sector appears to be impressive. Anyhow, maximisation of intra-port and inter-port competition still remains an area of concern.

To foster intra-port competition, the Government of India decided, in 1996, that major ports would become landlord ports and cargo-handling services would be privatised. Still, not much has happened. Neither the Government of India nor the ports are conscious of the need to promote competition. In fact, more than once, the Government has lost the opportunity to create intra-port competition. For instance, in Chennai, the Government put out all the (six) container berths in one bid instead of dividing them among two or more operators, which resulted in one party getting the facility for all six berths. In the process, the Government lost the opportunity to introduce intra-port competition.

It must also be pointed out that in the present dispensation, where Port Trusts are the owners and also service providers, they are called upon to introduce competition, or put out some of their facilities for private handling, and face competition from them. This, in fact, gives ports (as owners as well as service providers) an opportunity to discriminate against competing service providers. These issues can only be addressed at the policy level, and not by the regulator.

Monopolies elsewhere also influence pricing and competition within the country. For example, P&O Australia runs the container terminal facility in Kalang (Malaysia), Colombo, Karachi, Nhava Sheva (JNPT), and Chennai. They had also bid for Cochin, but looking at their monopoly in the region, the Government did not allow them to bid. Nonetheless, by operating facilities in and around India, they are still in a position to hike up rates in India or make operations in India difficult for others.

The Government, while inviting bids, should look at the existing operations of the bidder to ensure that a monopoly does not emerge. The European Commission does this on a regular basis. In one such case, the European Commission did not allow Hutchinson Whampoa of Hong Kong to enter into the Rotterdam Port because they were already controlling about 35 per cent of container handling facilities in Europe.

There are moves towards business consolidation, as shipping firms want to enter port operations. While this may be termed as vertical integration, there are fears that this would lead to extension of monopoly power.

Recently, the JNPT granted the third container terminal operation to a consortium of Maersk and Concor. While Maersk is the world's biggest shipping company, Concor is India's monopoly rail service provider for container movement. As of now, Maersk vessels carry about 30 per cent of India's containerised export-import cargo, and contribute to about 60 per cent share of the total box traffic handled by JNPT and Nhava Sheva Terminal. This development has raised fears that the terminal facility may turn into a captive facility instead of functioning as a common user facility.

Apart from the competition provided by the privately owned minor ports, there is very little competition in other ports. TAMP (Tariff Authority for Major Ports) has been set up, but it is not concerned about introducing competition. Besides, TAMP has no power to regulate terminal handling charges, by private operators, nor does it have the power to requisition records; summon or cross-examine witnesses; or even impose penalties for non-compliance.

And while there is a great private sector initiative, the fact is that most major ports have just one operator, and that is the port authority itself, i.e. the Government. It is difficult to see how efficiency levels can be raised unless genuine competition is allowed, and more private sector participation is allowed in the major ports. The way forward is to corporatise ports, but this too has been limited.

Railways

Introduced as early as 1853, Indian Railways has grown into one of the largest railway networks in the world. The network spread and expanded rapidly, and has become the principal mode of transport in the country. The Railways have also been modernised in terms of technology, ticketing, computerisation and overall management. This effort has been in tune with the requirement of moving large volumes of passenger and freight traffic.

Despite this, the share of the railways in traffic is declining with each passing year, to around 40 per cent today; while road traffic has grown by 12 per cent annually in the last decade, rail traffic has gone up only 1.4 per cent.

Indeed, freight rates have gone up faster than those for passengers, and the ratio of passenger to freight rates, at 0.32, is the lowest in the world. In the last ten years, the arrears in track renewal have increased from 3,500 km to more than 12,200 km, according to the Rakesh Mohan Committee on Railways. Partly due to this, and partly due to the supreme emphasis paid to passenger traffic, freight trains in India run at average speeds of 23 km an hour, as compared to an ideal required speed of 40-50 km, which is possible with modern locomotives and supporting infrastructure.

Competition Concerns in Railways

Presently, the Container Corporation of India (Concor) enjoys a monopoly over container movement by rail, to and from ports. Though, of late, Concor has failed to meet the growing demand for container movement in the country. A glaring example of this squeeze on availability, of containers, is provided by the recent congestion at JNPT, which handles nearly 60 per cent of India's container traffic. Despite adding to its existing fleet, the supply of rakes, by Concor, has been inadequate to meet the growing demand.

It can be argued that freight forwarders have the option of moving cargo by road. Notwithstanding, this involves either a down-payment of import duties when taking delivery of the goods, or furnishing of a bank guarantee in lieu, which is a costly process. On the contrary, the Government follows a discriminatory policy, if Concor is transporting the goods, the import duties can be paid at the final destination, i.e. the inland terminal. Thus, container movement via road becomes that much more uncompetitive, and serves to preserve the monopoly of Concor.

Given this, there seems to be need for the participation of other players in the container movement over rail. It is also realised that competition with Concor can become effective, only, if other operators are allowed to run container trains. In this context, the Government has recently taken a step to break the monopoly of Concor, by allowing the Pipavav Rail Corporation Ltd (PRCL) to transport containers by rail, on some 10 routes from Pipavav Port to all dry ports, including inland container depots. Interestingly, PRCL is a 50:50 joint venture between Pipavav Port in Gujarat and the Indian Railways.

Railway tracks constitute a natural monopoly. With the entry of other operators who would be using these tracks, there is a need to establish an independent regulatory authority to fix the prices and control the quality of supply. Furthermore, with the entry of other operators in container movement by rail, they will have to be allowed equal access to engines to pull these wagons. This requires a neutral regulator to ensure that the railways do not squeeze out competition by not allowing them to move their wagons.

With the road transport sector increasing its share in the total freight movement, there is a need for railway freight rates to become more flexible, so that they can respond to competition through periodic adjustments. Once the Golden Quadrilateral is in place, railways will face an increased competition from the road sector.

Road Transport

In recent times, the Government has laid great emphasis on the development of an adequate road network in the country. A vision of expressways, connecting the far corners of the country, has been projected. These projects may cost more than Rs 25,000 crore (nearly US$6 bn). It is undeniable that this vital infrastructure requirement would have to be developed with the private sector's participation.

The Indian road network, of nearly 3 million kilometres (kms), is one of the largest in the world. While the total length of the national roads network has increased 3.4 times, between 1951 and 1995, the total vehicle fleet has grown from 0.3 mn in 1951, to 12.5 mn in 1998, and is currently estimated at 22 mn.

Competition Concerns in Road Transportation

In the transportation of goods via trucks, most of the 22mn trucks plying on Indian roads are under single ownership, and there are few large-fleet operators. Although there appears to be competition, given the large number of truck owners, the fact is that about 5000 cargo operators handle the entire cargo. According to industry sources, in only about 2-3 per cent of cases, do customers directly access the truck owners and book their goods. The cargo operators cartelise and decide the freight, and there is no competition at their level. One way to break this cartelisation is by encouraging large fleet owners. However, restrictive provisions in the laws, relating to truck drivers, impair the formation of large fleets.

There are also instances of cartelised operations of the truckers' unions around major production sites and factories (see chapter on State Government Policies and Competition).

Another anti-competitive practice followed, this time in the name of the truckers, is by states, which fix minimum freight rates. How much this lowers competition can be seen from the fact that, when this was fixed at around Rs 11.50 per tonne kilometre in West Bengal two years ago, the transporters association there protested and said the measure would be inflationary! At that time, they paid the truckers around Rs 6.00 per tonne kilometre.

Increased competition in the road sector will require stopping state governments from issuing over-loading permits, or even fixing minimum freight rates. Encouraging larger fleet consolidation should also be the accepted policy principle.

In the construction of highways, the National Highways Authority has not taken steps to introduce competition in the market, for example, by structuring the bid documents in an appropriate way. Generally, bids are structured in a way, which allows only a few large players to bid. For example, if certain flyovers and bridges are to be built, then all of them are put in the same tender. Though two-three players bid, more often, the one who is awarded the contract, sub-contracts the work to the other remaining players – the so-called competitors. This was brought to light in the case of the Chennai flyover scam that had rocked the state assembly during the late 90's.

The Way Forward

There is no regulator in the transport sector, as in electricity, telecom or financial services. There is TAMP for the ports sector, but its role is confined to fixing port tariffs, and is not concerned about issues relating to efficiency or taking measures to create competition in the sector. For this reason, whatever needs to be done in the transport sector, to make it more competitive, has to be done by way of policy reforms. Since transport is inter-modal, the creation of a single super regulator could also be explored. Measures to introduce competition need to be taken by the Government at the policy level, as a major player in the transport sector, and not by the regulator. This is where perhaps the Competition Commission of India can play an active role-in influencing thinking, in the Government, on how to introduce competition in the various transport sectors.

RECOMMENDATIONS

- Policy reforms at the government level are required to introduce competition in the transportation sector
- The Government, while inviting bids for port operations, should look at existing operations of the bidder to ensure that a dominance does not emerge
- Provide a level playing field between the public and private sector operators
- Make enabling changes in the law to encourage the operation of large fleet operators on Indian roads

Part VII

Competition Policy in Services

19

Competition and Regulation in Financial Services

SHUBHASHIS GANGOPADHYAY*
PRAVEEN MOHANTY#

Introduction

Competition in the financial sector is important for a number of reasons. First, as in the real-estate sector, competition enables product innovation, and the development and adoption of efficient practices, which manifest in the introduction of financial instruments with different risk-return profiles, to allow better risk management (or portfolio balancing) for the individual and other investors. Secondly, new financial products at low costs improve the efficiency of the 'real' sector. Benefits reaped by the non-financial sector include, among other things, an improved access to capital, cheaper credit and housing loans for consumers, a better match between the financing needs of deficit and surplus units, etc.

While market forces are the main determinants of competition, it is important to have regulatory institutions that ensure that these forces operate effectively, and are not circumvented or blocked by those participating in the market.

Since the initiation of reforms in 1991, the financial sector (covering banking, insurance, capital markets, asset management and pensions) has seen a fundamental shift in its institutional structure. This shift has been brought about by a greater emphasis on competition, regulatory framework, supervisory oversight, and transparency. As a result, the financial sector has grown, not only in size but also through innovative products, aimed at meeting the

* Director, India Development Foundation, Gurgaon

Prognosis Capital Advisor, India Development Foundation, Gurgaon

financial intermediation needs of different segments of the economy. As domestic reforms progressed, increasing integration with global markets became another catalyst for further reforms. This has given the policy makers the confidence to continue with the reform process, of reducing the government's presence in the sector; transferring power to independent regulators; and relying on market forces to chart new growth paths for the sector as well as for the economy.

Yet, there is still a long way to go. Despite the reforms and the resulting entry of the private sector, government-owned institutions continue to dominate banking, insurance, and pensions.

Banking

Prior to 1991, the Indian banking sector was over-regulated. Predominantly government-owned, interest rates on deposits and lending were administratively determined. The branch distribution policy had led to a number of inefficient branches in various regions of the country. For example, the nationalised commercial banks had a large presence in (non-viable) rural and semi-urban areas.

Reforms led to the entry of private sector banks; deregulation of interest rates; autonomy for public sector banks; and the regulatory authority, the RBI, moving towards arm's length monitoring, through the application and tightening of prudential norms related to capital adequacy, income recognition and asset classification, in accordance with international norms and improved disclosure practices. The impact is evident in branch automation, ATM networks, multiple banking channels, and product and service innovations. Bank boards now have greater autonomy in deciding on where branches will be opened, and which branches need to be closed or transferred, unless a region becomes completely uncovered by any bank.

Earlier, through state ownership of banks, the Government indulged in directed lending, financial repression and political influence. Now, even though there are state-owned banks, the introduction of private and foreign banks have resulted in more competition in the banking sector. Also, state-owned banks face less political influence and hard budget constraints, along with stricter income recognition and disclosure norms. A study of more than a 100 countries suggests that private control of banks, coupled with strict disclosure norms, performs best for stability in the banking sector.

The benefits of reforms are the most pronounced in retail banking (households and the small sector) with a number of new products, such as vehicle loans, personal loans, housing or mortgage loans and credit cards. On the other hand, rural markets are yet to be adequately covered. The housing loan market has fuelled the construction sector, by generating employment and boosting other sectors, like steel and cement.

Wholesale banking, catering to large firms, has also witnessed new products like rupee interest rate swaps, forward rate agreements, interest rate futures, and foreign currency options. The interest rate and currency derivatives have experienced greater liquidity and 'finer' pricing, due to the entry of a large number of banks into such activities. Corporate customers have gained from these changes as they can now hedge their interest rate and currency risks; and hence, have greater flexibility in determining the conditions, under which they borrow. After all, wholesale banking is yet to match the spectacular growth achieved by retail banking, due to the debt recovery laws (or bankruptcy laws) that are still governed, by a misplaced emphasis on protecting current industries at the expense of the growth of new ones.

Insurance

Prior to the opening up of private participation in August 2000, the insurance sector was a government monopoly consisting of Life Insurance Corporation (LIC) and General Insurance Corporation (GIC) with its four subsidiaries. Now, there are 13 new life insurance companies and 8 new general insurance companies, mostly joint ventures with major global insurance players. The reform process has enhanced competition; provided more choices to the customer; triggered innovations; allowed various sorts of insurance packages; improved the efficiency levels; increased coverage in terms of density and penetration; obligated the insurers to provide for the needs of the rural and socially disadvantaged sectors; and increased the awareness among customers; as a result feeding the growth in the demand for insurance.

Even though, by international standards, the Indian insurance sector is far behind in terms of its penetration. This is largely because of the lack of a knowledge base on risk factors. Another hindrance, to the faster growth of insurance, is the necessity to have larger capital bases in the private companies. Here, they are at a disadvantage *vis-à-vis* the government-owned companies, which, often, have a better portfolio of customers because of their national reach and depth. Making the LIC a corporate entity, under the Companies Act, would eliminate the implicit government guarantee, and would provide the insurance sector with a level playing field. Over and above, relaxing the foreign direct investment cap on private companies may help in quickly increasing the capital base.

Asset Management/Mutual Funds

The Unit Trust of India (UTI) was set up in 1963, under an Act of Parliament. The first non-UTI mutual fund was launched a quarter of a century later, in 1987, when the State Bank of India launched the SBI Mutual Fund, followed by some of the other public sector banks and insurance companies. Many foreign players set up joint ventures with private Indian partners. The total assets under management are more than Rs. 1.6 trillion. From nothing in 1993, today (in 10 years time) private sector funds and foreign fund joint ventures manage around 78 per cent of the industry's total assets.

Be that as it may, on an international scale, our mutual funds industry is still quite small. One of the major problems, faced by the Indian mutual fund industry, is that it has not been able to excite the common investor (despite falling interest rates on deposits). This has largely been due to the lack of awareness among investors, and the plethora of government tax-saving savings schemes.

Pension Funds

As a first step, the Government introduced a pension scheme for employees joining the Central Government from January 1, 2004, based largely on the recommendations of the Expert Committee, set up by the Ministry of Social Justice and Empowerment, whose main recommendation was to set up a market oriented pension fund in the private sector, regulated by a Pensions Authority. The fund would be free to invest in the stock market and would enjoy favourable tax treatment.

The new pension proposal has moved away from that of defined benefit, to one where the returns are market determined, and allows private fund managers to operate these funds. Furthermore, it is not trying to 'capture' these savings for government-run projects, implying that if the Government wants this money, it has to compete with all other demanders of finance in the market and, for this reason, pay the market price of capital.

Anyhow, the real issue is one of a regulatory structure that develops confidence in investors to put their money into pensions. One way of doing this is to ensure that pension funds offer a return corresponding to the long-term returns in the capital market. What has undone a good initiative, is a recent report fixing the number of fund managers to a maximum of six, with at least one public sector institution.

Non-Banking Financial Companies (NBFCs)

By the mid-90s, there were more than 40,000 NBFCs in India, including a mix of large and small companies in the unorganised sector. The RBI (Amendment) Act, 1997, is also the most comprehensive attempt at regulating NBFCs. The focus of the regulatory structure is to safeguard depositors, and, at the same time, allowing greater flexibility to NBFCs, so that they can help in the development of a diversified financial sector. Supervision is carried out through on-site inspection, off-site surveillance, reports from the NBFCs' statutory auditors, and market data. For those NBFCs that accept public deposits, the regulatory structure treats them as if they are similar to banks. Moreover, unlike banks, NBFCs are not allowed to sell demand deposits.

The question remains as to whether, for regulatory purposes, such NBFCs should be treated as banks. Given that banks sell demand deposits, they are open to an asset-liability mismatch. NBFCs do not have the possibilities of a 'run' on their deposits, which are, in any case, not payable on demand. To such a degree, where is the reason to regulate them, the same way as one would regulate a bank?

Conclusion

Banks and financial institutions (FIs) will have to play a big role in furthering investment and growth. As with most emerging markets, Indian stock markets are yet to develop to meet the equity requirements of start-up businesses. The private equity market exists in a limited form for certain businesses, but not for others, especially those in the infrastructure sector. Companies, consequently, tend to rely more on FIs to fund their investments.

Nevertheless, this increases the concentration of risk held by the FIs, and they reduce the risk by lending less, or demanding collateral from prospective borrowers. In particular, the demand for collateral prevents start-up firms from accessing the formal credit markets, more than it prevents the large and already established businesses. What is needed for a sustained growth rate are profitable ideas to be funded, not only from the big industrial houses, but also from other quarters. As long as FIs lend to risky projects, they will continue to unload their risks on to those who are more willing and capable of bearing them. It is in this context that credit derivatives can play an important role, and, recently, rules and regulations have been suggested for trade in credit derivatives.

Many view derivatives as risky instruments, particularly that of systemic risk exposure. They feel that regulated institutions should not jump into these activities without proper safeguards of a regulatory framework. This sort of reasoning can be counter-productive on two counts. First, the very basis of the view can be erroneous. To say that systemic risk exposure of derivatives is high, one must compare it with the risk of alternative financial structures that derivatives replace, rather than on any abstract, or absolute measure. Second, the desire to get regulations in place, before institutions can trade in derivatives, may have the same results that we had in product markets during the licence *raj*. That system hampered and delayed product and process innovations. Similarly, a "regulation, and hence, permission first" approach may result in Indian financial markets following the expertise and knowledge of the regulators, rather than being led by the creativity of the financial innovators.

Restricting derivatives only, and not other functionally equivalent alternatives, can actually increase the systemic risk exposure. Clearly, there is a need to move from the current emphasis on regulating institutions, to one of functional regulation. If only some of the institutions are regulated, it will result in some of these alternatives becoming more expensive than others, thus giving rise to unnecessary distortions. A robust regulatory framework, with independent market regulators, oversees the growth of financial markets. Be that as it may, given the interdependence of these markets, and the bundling or unbundling of risks in a manner that results in multiple regulators having jurisdiction over a particular investment offering, there is a need to ensure that there is an integrated policy framework underlying the regulatory institutions. As in the case of the United Kingdom, India should reduce the multiplicity of regulators – and create a super regulator – to ensure a common approach to regulation of the different segments of the financial sector.

Recovery of financial claims becomes especially important when we consider the major objective of financial markets – reallocating risk so that the capital can move to more efficient activities. An important element of this reallocation is contained in the bankruptcy laws, which, in principle, should enable the reallocation of the capital from inefficient to efficient activities.

RECOMMENDATIONS

- To consider the appointment of a super regulator for the whole financial sector, as in the UK.
- Build capacity of the regulatory authorities to deal with the changing environment of the global financial system.
- Regulatory approach should be led by the creativity of the financial innovators, rather than 'regulation and hence permission first' approach.
- An integrated policy framework, aimed at promoting credibility and investor confidence, should replace multiple regulators over a particular investment offering.
- Risk should be relocated to allow capital to move to more efficient activities by changing bankruptcy laws.
- Corporatisation of institutions like the LIC would eliminate implicit government guarantees, usher transparency and provide a level playing field to private players.

20

Competition and Professional Services

T.C.A. ANANT*

The Market for Professional Services

The concept refers to activities, occupations, or business of individuals that require specialised education, knowledge, and skills, and is predominantly intellectual. The key defining characteristic here is that the service, supplied through individuals, is highly *idiosyncratic in character*. As a consequence, the service purchased by one consumer is not the same as that of another. This feature of professional services then lays the ground for different types of market failure, which can be on account of either informational issues, both asymmetric and imperfect information, or externalities.

Information: The consumer, in professional services, often does not know her/his own needs, as in medicine or law. The customer needs the specialist to disclose both what is wrong, and what needs to do done about it. The service provider is important in both shaping the demand, and for methods of filling it. Hence, for instance, a doctor determines the patient's requirements as well as the specific formulation needed. The scope to provide misleading information arises due to this inherent information asymmetry.

Externalities: The concept, in economic terms, refers to those costs and benefits, which arise in a transaction but are borne by parties other than the buyer and seller. For this reason, for instance, in accounting services, the buyer of the service is the client firm and the provider is the accountant/accounting firm. The beneficiaries are the people who rely on these reports to make their investment decisions. The consequences of collusion between the buyer and seller, or poor

* Professor, Department of Economics, Delhi School of Economics, University of Delhi, Delhi

judgment on the service provider's part, can lead to serious consequences, as the recent example of Enron would indicate. Furthermore, the benefits to the firm from having a credible, honest accountant may be less than the gain from a collusive one.

These types of problems are then typically defined as the basis for market regulation/intervention. Nevertheless, the idiosyncratic nature of professional services now leads to the next level of difficulty. Conventional regulatory styles, by focusing on prices, technologies and rates of return, are clearly inappropriate. Since the nature of service is so idiosyncratic, pricing, except in some limited aspects of service provision, is clearly not practical. Additional specifications of technology and rates of return are similarly unproductive, as they are better suited for process activities. It is for this reason that, unlike other activities, a process of self-regulation marks this sector.

While there is no clear formal definition of self-regulation, it refers to things like codes of conduct, voluntary labelling initiatives, ethical and quality standards. Associations of professional service providers formulate the standards or codes. Sometimes these associations have legal sanction, as in the case of the Bar Council/Medical Council. In other cases, particularly in case of sub-specialties, they are voluntary.

Competition Issues in Self Regulation

Before entering into a discussion on the issues in this section, a general caveat and disclaimer is in order. The ethical codes and conduct rules framed by the associations, in general, have the effect of reducing professional misconduct, improving disclosure of information, and improving client and social welfare in general. The examples cited below are examples of restrictions, where the beneficial impact may be counter-balanced by competition concerns, which we will outline. It is not the case that such standards are unique to India. They have been, and are being, used in other countries as well. The critical issue is the need for a clear assessment of competitive impact. In some cases, the standards have been challenged and are in the process of being modified.

Entry

The professional associations have an obligation to protect consumers from unqualified and unskilled persons, masquerading as professional service providers. For this purpose, the associations seek to certify quality in their members. This is done in two ways. Some associations conduct their own examination, whereas others prescribe standards for training institutions, and accept all qualified students as members. Both types of solutions raise questions. On the one hand, standards for universities raise issues of enforcement; and the in-house solution raises concerns for excessive restrictions. A related concern is one of recognition of foreign qualifications.

Professionals are usually required to practice as individuals or in partnership with others in the same profession. The reason usually given for these prohibitions is to ensure the practitioner's personal responsibility to the client. The link, of this, to the cost of doing business is not adequately addressed. On the other hand, corporate forms of business have the advantage of raising funds, like equity. This question has been partly addressed by the idea of a limited liability partnership. Again, there appears to be no progress on this suggestion. The motivation and need for such reforms can be seen in the case of 'stock broking'. Stock-Brokers, until recently, were functioning as partnerships, regulated by a self-regulatory stock exchange. Shifting to corporatised service providers has played an important role in deepening and strengthening the stock exchanges. Whilst one should not generalise from such examples, it is useful to examine alternatives to institutional assumptions.

Similarly, there are explicit and implicit restrictions on the names that can be used in partnerships. There are also moves to explicitly restrict the use of foreign brand names. This antipathy to brand names has some quality and efficiency implications. As seen in the case of other goods and services, brand identities help in quality control and facilitate consumer choice and decision-making. In addition, since brand identity is long term, it promotes inter-temporal efficiency as well. The no-brand name strategy in India oddly creates a bias in favour of family or relational identities. The effect is to strengthen established family firms-over new entrants to the profession.

Advertising

There is a marked tendency for professional associations to restrict advertising by its members. On that account, the associations, for accountants, lawyers and doctors, discourage or restrict advertising.

These restrictions are justified on the ground of needing to protect the public from incompetent practitioners and from misleading information. The problem is in a world with un-informed consumers, restrictions on advertising have a number of anti-competitive effects. They restrict entry, as the absence of information favours established actors. There is also reduced price competition, and consumers are not adequately informed about specialists. All these encourage the potential for collusive behaviour and unethical practices.

In the US, in 1979, the Federal Trade Commission held that such restraints on the advertising of doctors violated the anti-trust laws. Similarly, in the UK, during the 1970s, a number of references on advertising restrictions were held to be anti-competitive by the Monopolies Commission.

Assumptions on the Nature of Practice

The ethical standards of Professional Conduct are formulated with certain assumptions about the nature of practice. Hence, for instance, in the legal profession, the standards are centred largely around the legal process. The effect of this approach, is that the standards do not appropriately or effectively regulate non-litigating lawyers and consultants. *Similarly, the medical standards view the profession where an individual doctor deals with his patient.* The standards are silent on the issue of group-care or corporate or institutional practice. A related concern is the embargo on multi-disciplinary practices. This is most marked in law and accounting. This limits creation of newer products. These assumptions either restrict innovation or leave emerging areas of the market poorly or completely un-regulated.

Regulatory Capture

One of the problems of self-regulation is, that since the regulated entity is in charge of the regulation process, the possibility of capture is enhanced. The possibility of this risk is borne out by examining one classic example: the resorting to frequent strikes by lawyers. See, for instance, the judgement of the Supreme Court of India in the case "Ex-Capt. Harish Uppal *versus* Union of India and Another [(2003) 2 SCC 45]." The court observed that the bar had not restrained the lawyers. The thrust of this example is to illustrate a widespread unethical practice, and the unwillingness of the bar to restrict or discipline the profession. In some cases, like strikes, in order to limit transfer of jurisdiction, the objective is not very different from cartels seeking to share the market. In fact, from the viewpoint of anti-trust, strikes by professional service providers have a flavour, which is similar to a refusal to deal. The larger debate is the quality and nature of the disciplinary process of the associations, and their willingness to address customer concerns.

The point is that whilst ethical standards seek to promote consumer welfare, there are elements, which have the potential to promote anti-competitive behaviour.

Experiences of Other Countries in Self Regulation

In the US, the anti-trust laws have been applied to the professions since the landmark Supreme Court decision in *Goldfarb versus Virginia.* Goldfarb established that the Sherman Act contained no exemption for the professions. Similarly in the UK, the anti-monopoly provisions of the competition law apply to professional service providers. In France, the *Conseil de la concurrence* has made it clear that professional organisation rules may not authorise violations of the rules of competition law, notably those against price fixing agreements. These examples can be extended. In addition to formal actions and investigations of practices in the professions, many OECD competition authorities have been active in advocating more liberal regimes, and intervening in official enquiries in the attempt to obtain changes in anti-competitive rules operated in certain professions. Consequently, in addition to its explicit regulatory function, the US Federal Trade Commission staff has submitted *amicus curiae* briefs to state and self-regulatory entities, on competition issues relating to a variety of professions, including accountants, lawyers and architects.

Conclusion

The point of this limited review, is to illustrate the potential for anti-competitive consequences from certain regulatory assumptions. Section 21 of the Competition Act provides for the possibility of statutory authorities, which would include professional regulators, as we have noted, to seek the advice of the Commission. A more pro-active Commission, by using its *suo-moto* powers to analyse anti-competitive behaviour, may make such advice-seeking more fruitful.

To boot, in case of regulatory capture or failure, the competition authority, through its powers to fine, may provide an additional disciplinary device.

Alternatively, the self-regulatory organisations could encourage co-regulation, i.e. when its own action fails, then another authority or the Government could take action against the offending practitioners. A second alternative is for a third, independent authority to be set up at the state level, which could enforce standards through a stick-and-carrot approach (see Chapter on State Government Policies and Competition). The advantage with an independent authority is that it will not be prone to regulatory capture.

RECOMMENDATIONS

- Competition Commission of India to engage in deeper study through public hearings, etc, and a dialogue with professional regulatory authorities for better market practices
- Co-regulation to be examined as a way forward to discipline self-regulated professions
- State level competition agencies to enforce standards of professional conduct *vis-à-vis* competition concerns

Part VIII

Competition Policy in New Economy Areas

21

Competition Issues in Information Technology Sector

K.J. JOSEPH*

Introduction

The Information Communication Technology (ICT) sector in India, employs about 0.6 million persons and creates approximately US$16 bn worth of wealth every year. Software and service exports from India recorded an annual compound growth rate of over 60 per cent, in rupee terms, and around 45 per cent in dollar terms, during the last decade. Despite adverse market conditions since 2001, India earned US$12.3 bn from exports in 2003-04. The share of software and service sector in total exports increased almost seven-fold (from 3.2 per cent to 21.3 per cent), during 1996-2003. This sector today accounts for over 2.6 per cent of India's GDP, as compared to 0.5 per cent in 1996-97.

India exports IT and IT-enabled services to over 180 countries and Indian firms, from both private and government sectors, are training people in IT in 55 countries. Over 100 of the 'Fortune 500' companies have set up R&D centres in India to utilise the IT potential of the country. The striking fact is that India's success has been achieved almost entirely by native firms.

Nevertheless, even today, the software and service sector is confined mainly to a few metropolitan cities, remaining as enclaves with limited linkages with the rest of the country, as growth of the sector was mainly fuelled by exports. The result is that India is still to emerge as a major user of ICT in the domestic sectors of the economy, which is important for the country, to enhance efficiency, productivity, and in improving international competitiveness.

---

* Visiting Senior Fellow, Research and Information System for the Non-Aligned and Other Developing Countries (RIS), New Delhi

Overview of the Sector

India has established credibility, in the international software and services market, on account of its better quality services, which, in turn, makes India an attractive location for the off-shoring of services.

India's exports are concentrated in the US market and are not diverse enough. In terms of the destination of exports, the US accounted for 67.8 per cent, followed by the UK with 14 per cent, in 2003-04. The share of Asian countries is estimated at about 8 per cent, of which the Japanese market accounts for almost 3 per cent.

The higher export growth during the 1990s notwithstanding, Indian firms, by and large, operate at the low end of the value chain. Indian firms, in general, fare poorly in terms of competence, profitability and value added per employee, as compared to the foreign firms.

Since 2001, the software exports' growth rate is declining. On the other hand, this period also witnessed the emergence of IT Enabled Services (ITES) as a major component of software and service exports from the country. The share of ITES, in the total industry's export more than doubled from about 14 per cent in 2000, to more than 29 per cent in 2003-04.

Development of India's IT Sector: Role of the State

The development of the IT sector was aided by the various policy initiatives and institutional interventions by the Government of India and state governments over the years. The Central Government, as far back as 1972, made provisions like the duty-free import of computer systems, 100 per cent foreign ownership, etc., to encourage software exports. The impetus from the Government was sustained over time. With the economic reforms of the 1990s, a major thrust was given to the software exports' sector through measures, like encouragement for foreign investment; greater private sector involvement in policy making; better finance opportunities; reduction and rationalisation of taxes, duties and tariffs; and infrastructure development for faster and cheaper data.

To meet the growing demand of software personnel due to the expansion of software development in India, and growing brain drain, the Government expanded the capacity of the higher education system, in engineering, by setting up new institutions.

A notable institutional intervention by the Government has been the establishment of Software Technology Parks (STP), in different states, to provide the necessary infrastructure for software exports. The units in the STPs account for about 80 per cent of the exports of software from the country. In June 2000, a new STP was set up in Silicon Valley, US, with a view to facilitate software exports by small and medium firms to the US.

Till recently, the weak copyright regime in the country facilitated the proliferation of software piracy, which, in turn, acted as a disincentive for firms to develop software products. To address this problem, the Government initiated a series of measures. The copyright of computer software has been protected under the provisions of Indian Copyright Act of 1957. Major changes were made to the copyright law in 1994, which made it illegal to make, or distribute copies, of copyrighted software. In addition, the Government, in co-operation with industry associations, conducts regular anti-piracy raids to discourage software piracy.

Software piracy in the country still remains at a high level, affecting software product development in the country. The incidence of the high level of piracy is due to the high prices of IT products in a developing country, like India. Like so, the incidence of piracy is likely to continue until there is a significant reduction in the price of software products. This, in turn, calls for promoting the development and use of open source software.

Role of Private Sector and Industry Associations

The industry associations and private sector have an equally important role, like the Government, in the development of the ICT sector in India. Industry associations, particularly the National Association of Software and Service Companies (Nasscom), played a key role to project India's image in the world market by lobbying abroad, and initiating the anti-piracy drives in India.

The policy reforms in the 1990s, which had the effect of liberalising trade and investment, facilitated the entry of a large number of foreign firms into India's ICT sector. Though the share of foreign firms, even today, accounts for only about 20 per cent of the total export, their presence in the Indian market seems to have had the effect of enhancing the credibility of Indian firms in the world market.

Despite the foundation provided by the Government, the industry could take off, only in the 1990s, with a high growth in world demand *inter alia* on account of the Y2K problem and greater participation by the private sector. India's IT success thus appears to be a typical case of proactive state intervention, with an active role for the private sector.

Structure of IT Market and Competition

The IT industry is a multi product industry comprising both hardware and software. IT hardware consists of a large number of products like computers, peripherals, network equipment, communication equipment, and so on. Similarly, in the case of software, there are software services and software products.

The computer industry in India has passed through different phases. In the 1960's, industry was dominated by foreign firms, whereas the 1970's was a period of public sector domination. The 1980's witnessed the emergence of private domestic firms dominating the industry. The liberalised policies of the 1990's, that removed the entry barriers to the foreign firms coupled with the emergence of the software boom, have had the following effects. First, many of the domestic hardware firms, like Wipro, HCL and others, who dominated the hardware sector during the 1980's have diversified into software and service exports. Secondly, with the opening of the domestic economy, today, all the world leaders in the hardware sector are present in the domestic market. Thirdly, with easy availability of SKD/CKD kits, with the removal of tariff barriers, there has been a mushrooming of the non-branded market.

According to the Manufacturers Association of Information Technology (MAIT), Indian brands account for 21 per cent, and the foreign firms share is 26 per cent. About 53 per cent of the market is accounted for by the non-branded market[1].

Thus, there appears to be strong competition between three major sets of actors. The foreign firms have been able to increase their share, and almost all the leading players in the world market, like DELL,

1. See for details http://www.mait.com/industry.asp

IBM, Acer, HP etc., are present in the domestic market. Though there are a large number of domestic firms in the field, none of them appears to be enjoying a dominant position. In fact, it could be argued that the presence of a strong non-branded sector, accounting for more than 50 per cent of the total market, acts as a major factor in creating a highly competitive market structure.

The presence of a competitive market structure is evident from the fact that the high growth recorded, during 2002-03, has been an outcome of reduced customs duties, which in turn was passed on to the consumers, in the form of lower prices. Had the industry not been competitive, the effect of reduced duty structure would not have been reflected in the prices.

Computer hardware today, however, is a relatively less important segment of the IT industry. The more important segment, which facilitates the harnessing of new technology for development, is the software. The software, in turn, could be broadly divided into operating systems and applications software, either taking the form of software services, or products. Each of these product segments has varying market structures and competitive environment.

In case of the operating systems, it is well known that a single firm in the world dominates the market for it. Microsoft operating system 'windows' controls over 90 per cent of the desktop software market. Lack of competition in this crucial segment, in turn, has its effect not only on the price at which it is available, but also sets limits on the development of application software, based on this operating system, because of the lack of access to source codes. Both of these factors, when interacting with each other, lead to a situation wherein the new technology is made inaccessible to the domestic market of a country, like India with low per capita income-leading to low domestic demand. The high price of software also induces software piracy, which in turn dampens any effort at development of software products for the domestic market.

At the same time, the Indian ICT firms, given these constraints and having the option of either focusing on the local or foreign market, naturally opted for the booming foreign market. Also, the state policies and institutional interventions provided a highly conducive environment for the exploitation of export opportunities. Thus, the increased export orientation (mostly catering to the high income countries that could afford the high price of software), and the neglect of the domestic market by the Indian ICT firms, has to be seen in the context of the existing market structure and competitive environment.

India's software service sector consists of over 3000 firms and appears to present a long tailed distribution; wherein 7 firms in 2002-03 are found to be having an export of over 1000 crore, whereas 2644 firms were found to be too small [with an export of less than 10 crore, (see Table 21.1)].

Table 21.1

Size Distribution of Indian Software Firms (2002-2003)

Size Class (in crore)	*No. of Firms*	*Share in Total*
Less than 10	2644	87.23
10 to 50	244	8.05
50 to 100	73	5.71
100 to 250	43	1.40
250 to 500	15	0.49
500 to 1000	5	0.16
More than 1000	7	0.23
Total	**3031**	**100.00**

Source: Nasscom, 2004

It is also found that the share of the top four firms in exports is only about 26 per cent, and even the top 19 firms account for about 40 per cent of the total exports. Given the fact that Indian firms are mostly export-oriented, and they have to compete with large multinational firms, there appears to be the need for reaping scale economies to remain competitive. This, in turn calls for consolidation such that Indian firms are able to enhance international competitiveness, and also able to venture into risky and investment incentive areas, like software products. The recent trend, in terms of the incidence of a large number of mergers and takeovers, is to be seen in the context of the industry's attempt at consolidation. Our inquiry has shown that since 2003, 19 foreign firms were taken over by Indian firms; there were 13 cases of acquisition between Indian firms, and foreign firms acquired 8 Indian firms.

The open source, or free[2] software, movement is an attempt at making the software segment more competitive, and promotes the development application software. India, being a country with abundant supply of skilled manpower, is well endowed to promote the development of open source software. But, as in the case of most products, demand constraint is bound to set limit to such initiatives. In such context, if the past experience is any indication, the government policy could play a significant role, which could make the software segment more competitive in structure.

Firstly, from the software side, the state policy should explicitly promote the use of open source software, and provide special incentives for such projects. Secondly, for promoting domestic use of new technology, it is worthwhile to consider development of software for domestic use on par with any innovative activity, and receive all the incentives enjoyed by firms undertaking in-house R&D, for the development of new products or processes. Thirdly, from the hardware side, there are innovations, like simputer, that need to be further encouraged, such that the hardware price could be brought down further.

Conclusion

The unprecedented growth performance of the IT sector (in terms of its export earning) not withstanding, the use of this technology in the domestic economy appears to be less remarkable.

In case of hardware, with the removal of entry barriers, almost all the leading players in the world market have a presence in India. The removal of tariff barriers and the presence of a large non-branded market, act as sources of increased competition. The situation appears to be different in case of software. The high market concentration in some of the software segment, especially in operating systems, seems to have the effect of making software high priced, but also dampens the development of applications software on account of the lack of access to source codes. The high price tends to make software beyond

2. Stallman clarifies that the word 'free' pertains to freedom not price. "You may or may not pay for a program," he says. "Either way, once you have the software you have three freedoms – first, the freedom to copy the program and give it away to friends and co-workers; second, the freedom to change the program, by having the full source code; third, the freedom to distribute an improved version and thus help build this community." See for details, http://www.networkmagazineindia.com/200108/inperso2.htm

the reach of many, and adversely affects demand. In addition, it also promotes software piracy, which acts as a major disincentive for the development of software for the domestic market. These factors, along with lack of inducement mechanisms to induce the IT firms to exploit the domestic market, has had the effect of limited use of IT in other sectors of the economy.

Given the fact that the state played a proactive role, so far, in the development of IT and software service sectors in the economy, active state involvement is called for. A more competitive environment in the software sector can be created by promoting the open source software. Towards this end, the state could provide appropriate incentives for the promotion of open source software, and create demand by promoting its use in all the e-governance projects. In addition, the incentives and concessions offered to the export market may be extended to those firms developing software for the domestic market as well, such that the Indian ICT firms work together with other sectors of the economy and develop the needed domain expertise. From the hardware side, the innovations, like simputer, need to be encouraged, such that hardware becomes more affordable and thus leads to greater demand.

RECOMMENDATIONS

- Encourage consolidation, in the form of M&As, to weed out sub-optimal operations in the industry.
- Provide incentives for firms to develop software for the domestic market.
- Government policy should promote the use of open source software to increase the affordability of ICT in the domestic sector.
- Indigenous innovations like 'simputer' should be encouraged to bring down the hardware prices.

22

Implications of Competition Policy on Biotechnology Industry in India

A. DAMODARAN*

Introduction

India's biotechnology (BT) sector is emerging as one of the fastest growing industries, reckoned in terms of the volumes of investment attracted in recent years. During 2003-04, India's biotech sector is estimated to have attracted private investments to the tune of US$140 mn. Infrastructure and R&D account for nearly 80 per cent of these investments. The two significant factors, that lie at the base of India's biotechnology potential, are the scientific and technical pool of human resources, and the rich biodiversity of the country.

With an interesting demographic profile, and a large agriculture sector, India also affords a large market base for new biotechnology products. The industry is made up of around 235 companies, the majority of which commenced operations after 1999. In terms of their presence, the bio-pharma sector accounted for 76 per cent of the biotech industry, followed by bio-services (8.5 per cent), bio-industrial (7.5 per cent), bio-agri (5.5 per cent), and bio-informatics (2 per cent). The bio-services sector includes clinical research and related, contracted, research programmes.

It is estimated that India's market size for biotech products and services would attain a level of US$1.5 bn in 2007, and would leap to US$4.5 bn by 2010. Exports of biotech products would add another US$4.5 bn, making India's biotech industry a US$9 bn giant by 2010. India has acquired competence in the areas of bioprocess engineering; downstream processing and isolation methods; bio-material extracts;

* Professor, Indian Institute of Management (IIM), Bangalore. The author acknowledges use of data from Biospectrum

re-combinant DNA technology, and in the fabrication of bio-processing equipments, including bio-reactors.

Biotechnology Policies in India

Though biotechnology has been a major sector in India for over two decades, there is no National Policy on biotechnology so far. A few years ago, the Department of Biotechnology (DBT), the nodal agency of the government, had formulated a 10-year vision document on biotechnology. Due to persistent demand from the industry for a cohesive national outlook on this important sector, the Government is currently evolving a National Biotech Policy. The policy is most likely to be made public in January 2005.

The vision document emphasises the significance of private-public partnerships to provide a major fillip to the growth of the biotechnology industry in India. Infusion of foreign investments and formation of joint ventures are amongst strategies outlined in the national policy paper. The DBT forms the nodal point for policy formulation and programme implementation in the sector. This Department was set up in 1985 and has, since then, undertaken major programmes for human resource and infrastructure development for the biotech sector. The Department has set up a technology development fund for the development of Small and Medium Enterprises (SMEs), which is expected to supplement private venture capital funds in promoting promising micro-enterprises.

It is envisaged that during the 10th Five Year Plan, a large number of SMEs would be promoted, through enabling financial infrastructure created by the Department of Biotechnology, focussing especially on agri-biotech products. The efforts of the Department are supplemented by programmes undertaken by the Indian Council of Agriculture Research (ICAR); the Council of Scientific and Industrial Research (CSIR); the Indian Council of Medical Research (ICMR); and the Department of Science and Technology. Notable private and public R&D institutes, such as the Indian Institute of Science, the Tata Institute of Fundamental Research; and state government-sponsored R&D institutes, such as the Institute for Bio-informatics and Applied Biotechnology (IBAB), in Karnataka, have also played a major role in the development of research programmes.

Apart from national policies and programmes, state governments have also initiated major policy, and industrial support, programmes to encourage biotechnology. Notable states, which have taken the lead in this regard are, Andhra Pradesh, Karnataka and Maharashtra. The sub-national policies are focussed on providing physical infrastructure and financial support for developing biotech clusters, based on close twinning of R&D institutes with start-up firms, that would commercialise technologies churned out by the former.

One of the most interesting features of India's biotech sector is the keen sub-national competition for attracting investments and industrial units. Andhra Pradesh, Karnataka and Maharashtra are locked in keen competition to advertise their industrial support mechanisms, in order to attract units both from within the country and outside. The focus of the competition is on pre-production facilities, that enable new units to leverage external economies, for attaining an edge in production and operational capacities.

The States of Karnataka and Andhra Pradesh have tried to exploit their IT potential to attract IT-BT fusion projects, notably in the area of bio-informatics. There have also been interesting efforts to attract knowledge-intensive enterprises through other enabling means. For example, the State Government of Maharashtra has gone a step further to set up biotech parks in Pune to house pilot plant facilities that could be used by biotech companies on lease basis, without having to make capital investments. This is in addition to the State's efforts to make forays in bio-informatics and bio-processing. Still, these efforts suffer from absence of leveraging effects, and bias towards bio-informatics.

Backward Integration through Joint Ventures, Mergers and Acquisitions (M&As)

In the developed world, joint ventures, and mergers and acquisitions are commonplace occurrences, particularly in the biotech sector. Very often, M&As are motivated by the desire to monopolise market share, and avoid competition. When it comes to acquisitions, the situation could display unusual trends, and may be motivated by more than one consideration. Thus, General Electric (GE), which was a leading manufacturer of machines, such as Positron Emission

Tomography and MRI scanners, acquired all outstanding shares of Amersham, which had expertise as a leading player in the market for scanners and contrast drugs used in X-rays, CT scans, Ultrasound, MRI and PET scans. Through the acquisition, GE's strategy was to create a health care company, which could have a dominant position in common markets. More importantly, GE considered the deal to help it leverage the knowledge base of Amersham in the use of gene therapy for treating patients, and thus more effectively compete with Roche and Abbot Laboratories, the leading diagnostic and drug firms in the world.

Mergers and acquisitions, in the biotech sector in India, will depend upon the functioning of the new Competition Act of 2002. There exists potential for mergers and acquisitions, amongst subsidiaries of multinational companies that are functioning in India, particularly in the bio-pharma, agri-biotech and bio-supplier segments. Nevertheless, Indian firms and R&D establishments definitely look forward to transferring their innovations to firms, through the joint venture route. Publicly funded institutions, such as the Central Drug Research Institute, are also not averse to having collaborations with overseas entities, including multinational corporations, especially in the field of joint research. In the agri-biotech sector, the Indian Agricultural Research Institute (IARI) has already entered into a successful tie-up with The Energy & Resources Institute (TERI), New Delhi and has been working with multinationals, such as Syngenta, to develop markets for third generation biotech products, including transgenics.

Regulatory Regime for Biotech Industry in India

Multiple regulatory authorities deal with biotechnology products and processes in India. This will be evident from the following.

Regulatory Framework:

As far as the agri-biotech is concerned, the following form the principal regulatory agencies and legislations:

a. Ministry of Agriculture/ICAR
   - Plant Variety and Farmers Rights Act, 2002
   - Seeds Act, 1966

- Plants, Fruits and Seeds (Regulation of Import into India) Order, 2003

b. Ministry of Health

- Prevention of Food Adulteration, Act

c. Ministry of Environment and Forests

- National Biodiversity Legislation, 2002
- Rules for Manufacture, Use, Import, Export and Storage of Hazardous Micro-organisms and Genetically Engineered Organisms or Cells, 1989 which form the bio-safety regulations flowing from the Environment Protection Act, 1986.

In 2003, a National Task Force was set up under the chairmanship of Dr M S Swaminathan, to formulate a new regulatory structure for bio-agri products. The Task Force submitted its report in May 2004 and the Government is in the process of implementing the suggestions, after consulting all the stakeholders. The Swaminathan Task Force has essentially suggested the formation of a single agency, the National Biotechnology Regulatory Board, on the lines of the Space Commission, Telecom Commission, and Atomic Energy Regulatory Board etc., to be run by professionals. The Board should have permanent members who specialise in various subjects of biotechnology, and all the existing regulations will need to be harmonised to provide a single window system for biotech products.

Following this, the Government had set up another Task Force under the chairmanship of Dr R A Mashelkar (Director General, CSIR), to simplify the regulatory procedures for recombinant pharma products. The Mashelkar Task Force report is awaited.

India's Competition Act, 2002

India has enacted a new competition law, the Competition Act (2002) to (a) prevent practices having adverse effects on competition (b) promote and sustain competition in markets (c) protect the interests of consumers, and (d) look into factors that suppress freedom of trade carried out by other participants in markets in India. To this extent, the Act goes beyond a narrow consumer focussed vision that is typical of competition policies in certain other parts of the world. It is also noteworthy that despite the legacy of the

Monopolies and Restrictive Trade Practices (MRTP) Act of 1969, the Competition Act (2002) is not obsessed by the desire to prevent firms from protecting or expanding, their market shares by non-efficiency factors. Finally, the Act also provides for advocacy whereby other branches of Government would need to respond to such advice, so as to least interfere with market competition.

The Act defines an enterprise as: including a person or a department of the Government that is engaged in any activity, that is related to production, storage, supply, distribution, acquisition or control of articles of goods. Section 3 (1) of the Act, by prohibiting anti-competitive agreements that are non-efficient in nature, sends an important signal to the biotechnology community in India that would like to practice the 'terminator' or 'generic use restriction technologies'. Similarly, Section 4 of the Act, by restricting abuse of dominant position by an enterprise, has the capacity to prevent chances of predatory or unfair pricing of seeds or drugs, as the case may be. Section 4 (2) (b), by excluding limitations or restrictions of goods and services that are favourable to consumers or public interest, provides greater legitimacy to the compulsory licensing provisions in the Patents Act, 1970 (as amended in 2002), and the Plant Varieties and Farmers' Rights Act of 2001. Section 5 (b) of the Competition Act also prevents acquisitions that are restrictive in impacts on market access, and thus could play an important role in predatory acquisitions in the biotech sector. This is, however, subject to the financial thresholds specified (see chapter on Mergers & Acquisitions in India).

Competition Issues

Competition issues in the biotech field would mainly arise from the application of Intellectual Property Rights over biotech products, by innovating companies. The phenomena of mergers and acquisitions would be the second important competition issue that may arise in India's biotech industry. Both aspects would encourage monopoly rights in production, distribution and marketing of biotech products. This would, in turn, impact on the consumers of biotech products, through higher pricing of products and restrictions on its multiplication. Yet, the presence of public plant biotech research institutions, that seek to position their products according to local conditions, could dampen the oligopolistic tendencies. Even in the bio-pharma sector, the trend towards seeking joint ventures in research needs to be welcomed, as it would serve to encourage joint commercial ventures in future.

Similarly, in the bio-pharma sector, India's Patent Act (1970), as modified through the first and second amendments, can adversely affect the ability of generic drug manufacturers to adopt alternative processes to develop new drugs, in view of the product patent regime that would be fully operational by 1st January 2005. Even the interim exclusive marketing right regime, which is currently operational, acts to virtually confer monopolistic rights, over distribution and marketing of new drugs, for which product patents have been obtained in PCT (Patent Co-operation Treaty) countries.

Under the Plant Varieties and Farmers' Rights Act (2001) that confers plant breeders rights for new, distinct, uniform and stable varieties; farmers' rights to sell produce originating from protected varieties is not allowed. To this extent, it would be possible for plant biotechnology companies, producing non-hybrid varieties of plants or seeds, to enforce full-cost and high margin pricing systems for seeds that are considered essential for farming operations.

Flexibilities in India's IPR Regimes and its Impact on Competition

Notwithstanding the IPRs conferred through the Indian Patent Act, and the Plant Varieties and Farmers Rights Act of 2002, which *prima-facie* confer significant economic exclusiveness to producers of new biotech products and process; it is a plain fact that these IPR regimes have the potential for extreme cases of competition restriction. Accordingly, the Patent (Amendment) Act of 2002 provides the flexibilities of abridging rights of inventors, whose primary or intended use or commercial exploitation of their invention would be contrary to public order or morality, or causes serious prejudice to human, animal or plant life, or health, or to the environment.

The Act is also notable for its opposition provisions and for its requirement on the part of a potential inventor, to disclose source and geographic origin of the biological material used in an invention. This clause, which is incorporated in Section 10 of the said Act, fortifies the 'prior consent' principle, enshrined in India's National Biodiversity Act, 2002. Under the Plant Varieties and Farmers' Rights Act of 2001, the Central Government reserves the right to enforce compulsory licencing of protected varieties and seeds, in the larger interest of food security, livelihood and consumer welfare.

To the extent that these flexibilities exist, it may be fair to surmise that the Indian IPR regimes do promote, or facilitate, a healthy competition culture. It also follows that there is an implicit effort to coordinate the objectives of India's competition law with that of the country's IPR regimes, particularly in relation to biotechnology. It is quite possible, therefore, to ensure that IPR rules do not act as a threat to competition concerns, in the biotechnology sector.

To conclude, India's fast growing biotech sector has the potential of serious implications on the competition environment in the country. Be that as it may, a constellation of pro-active legislation serves to ensure that competition is not impaired. India's IPR regimes, while affording protection to inventions that fulfil the criteria of novelty, non-obviousness and commercial application, do still carry with it the elements for regulating anti-competitive behaviour, on the part of the firms concerned. The flexibilities inherent in India's IPR regimes, coupled with bio-safety, biodiversity and stringent food safety laws, could go a long way in promoting the biotech sector, in a manner that is sustainable and economically advantageous.

RECOMMENDATIONS

- The Government needs to establish a Biosafety Regulatory Board at the earliest
- The Competition Commission will have to gear up in dealing with competition issues in the sector, due to the weak coverage on IPRs in the Competition Act, 2002
- The Government should also examine how the extant IPR laws can deal with competition problems, which may arise due to abuse of dominance

THE STEERING COMMITTEE

Towards a Functional Competition Policy for India (FunComp Project)

S. Sundar, *Distinguished Fellow,* The Energy and Resources Institute (TERI), New Delhi	Chairman
Shankar Acharya *Honorary Professor,* Indian Council for Research on International Economic Relations (ICRIER), New Delhi	Member
T.C.A. Anant *Professor,* Dept. of Economics, Delhi School of Economics, University of Delhi, Delhi	Member
Suman Bery *Director General,* National Council of Applied Economic Research (NCAER), New Delhi	Member
B.B. Bhattacharya *Director,* Institute of Economic Growth, Delhi	Member
S. Chakravarthy *Adviser/Consultant* Competition Policy and Law, and *Fellow* CUTS-Centre for Competition, Investment & Economic Regulation (C-CIER)	Member
V.K. Dhall *Member* Competition Commission of India New Delhi	Special invitee
Subhashis Gangopadhyay *Director,* India Development Foundation (IDF), Gurgaon	Member
Subir Gokarn *Chief Economist* CRISIL Ltd., New Delhi	Member

Contd. ...

Pradeep S. Mehta *Secretary General* CUTS International	Member
Shrawan Nigam *Adviser* Planning Commission, Government of India	Member
Manoj Pant *Professor* School of International Studies, Jawaharlal Nehru University, New Delhi	Member
T.C.A. Srinivas Raghavan *Consulting Editor* Business Standard, New Delhi	Member
S.L. Rao *Chairman* Institute for Social and Economic Change (ISEC), Bangalore	Member
Pronab Sen *Adviser* Planning Commission, Government of India	Member